TAKING ON THE B.E.S.T

4TH GRADE MATH

STUDENT WORKBOOK

MISTAKES ARE PROOF YOU'RE TRYING

A high-energy math program aligned specifically to Florida's B.E.S.T. Standards for Math

Video Lessons with Ms. McCarthy

Extra Practice to Promote Student Growth

Math Tasks, Error Analysis & More

Created by Sarah McCarthy

HEY WORLD CHANGER!

I just wanted to take a moment to introduce myself. My name is Ms. McCarthy, and I am so excited to be a part of your math journey this year. My mission is to make math FUN, make it CLICK, and make it STICK for you. I will be there to support you by walking you through the skills and tools you will need to be successful in math this year, but that will only take you so far.

You see, your willingness to try and persistence to keep going even when it gets tough will be the keys to your success . I challenge you to take charge of your learning and stick with each math skill until you get it. Think you can handle that? I believe in you and know that you can do this!

Go ahead and commit to learning and growing this year by filling out the statement below:

I, _____, hereby make a sincere commitment to give this school year everything I've got. I will take charge of my learning by asking questions and solving problems to the best of my ability. When work is challenging for me, I will stay determined and stick with it until I get it.

Sign your name: X _____

Way to go! Let's get to it, and "LET ME TEACH YA!"

- Ms. McCarthy

"TAKING ON THE B.E.S.T."
Theme Song

Do you know what the BEST version of you looks like?
Just take a look in the mirror,
The person that you were born to be and say,
"I'M TAKING ON THE BEST!"

Every day is a new day to step it up
And maybe some days I feel like giving up
I just don't get it,
but I can't forget
That I'm a believer in the POWER OF YET!

I may not know it now, but I will
Take a deep breath, and I'm chill
Mistakes are part of the game,
I embrace 'em
I don't run from my fears,
I face 'em

How?
I pay attention
I take charge of my learning
Draw it out, and work it out
To show my journey
Try until it clicks,
Make sure that it sticks,
Working at it constantly is my secret

Practice is not something I do once I'm good
It's the one thing I do that makes me good
So I take another step
I'm obsessed with progress
You know why? (Why?)
I'M TAKING ON THE BEST!

MATHEMATICAL
Mindset Creed

THIS IS A SAFE PLACE TO MAKE MISTAKES.
Mistakes help me learn and grow.

I AM A HARD WORKER.
I stick with it until I get it.

I AM BRAVE. I TAKE CHARGE OF MY LEARNING.
I ask questions when I don't understand.

WHEN IN DOUBT, I DRAW IT OUT (IF POSSIBLE).
And it's always possible to work it out.

I RESPECT AND ACTIVELY LISTEN
To the ideas of others.

NOTES

_____
_____
_____
_____
_____
_____
_____
_____

TABLE OF CONTENTS

(MA.4.NSO.1.2 continues on next page)

Video lessons can only be viewed with a membership at McCarthyMathAcademy.com

TABLE OF CONTENTS

Video lessons can only be viewed with a membership at McCarthyMathAcademy.com

TABLE OF CONTENTS

Video lessons can only be viewed with a membership at McCarthyMathAcademy.com

TABLE OF CONTENTS

(MA.4.NSO.2.3 continues on next page)

Video lessons can only be viewed with a membership at McCarthyMathAcademy.com

TABLE OF CONTENTS

(MA.4.NSO.2.5 continues on next page)

Video lessons can only be viewed with a membership at McCarthyMathAcademy.com

TABLE OF CONTENTS

(MA.4.NSO.2.7 continues on next page)

Video lessons can only be viewed with a membership at McCarthyMathAcademy.com

TABLE OF CONTENTS

Video lessons can only be viewed with a membership at McCarthyMathAcademy.com

TABLE OF CONTENTS

(MA.4.FR.1.3 continues on next page)

Video lessons can only be viewed with a membership at McCarthyMathAcademy.com

TABLE OF CONTENTS

(MA.4.FR.2.1 continues on next page)

Video lessons can only be viewed with a membership at McCarthyMathAcademy.com

TABLE OF CONTENTS

Video lessons can only be viewed with a membership at McCarthyMathAcademy.com

TABLE OF CONTENTS

TABLE OF CONTENTS

Video lessons can only be viewed with a membership at McCarthyMathAcademy.com

TABLE OF CONTENTS

TABLE OF CONTENTS

TABLE OF CONTENTS

Video lessons can only be viewed with a membership at McCarthyMathAcademy.com

TABLE OF CONTENTS

(MA.4.GR.1.2 continues on next page)

Video lessons can only be viewed with a membership at McCarthyMathAcademy.com

TABLE OF CONTENTS

TABLE OF CONTENTS

TABLE OF CONTENTS

Video lessons can only be viewed with a membership at McCarthyMathAcademy.com

TAKING ON THE B.E.S.T.

Video Lesson **Foundational Skills**

PLACE VALUE

2	1	9	,	3	0	8

VALUE OF DIGITS

2	2	0	,	0	7	7

23

© McCarthy Math Academy

TAKING ON THE B.E.S.T.

MA.4.NSO.1.1 | Video Lesson | **10 Times Greater**

---

1 Write the number 47,513 in the place value chart below.

Hundred thousands	Ten Thousands	Thousands	Hundreds	Tens	Ones

Write a number that has the digit 5 in a place that is ten times greater than digit 5 in 47,513.	
Write a number that has the digit 1 in a place that is ten times greater than digit 1 in 47,513.	
Write a number that has the digit 7 in a place that is ten times greater than digit 7 in 47,513.	

---

2 Write the number 98,234 in the place value chart below.

Hundred thousands	Ten Thousands	Thousands	Hundreds	Tens	Ones

Write a number that has the digit 8 in a place that is ten times greater than digit 8 in 98,234.	
Write a number that has the digit 4 in a place that is ten times greater than digit 4 in 98,234.	
Write a number that has the digit 2 in a place that is ten times greater than digit 2 in 98,234.	

24

TAKING ON THE B.E.S.T.

| Extra Practice #1 | 10 Times Greater

1 Write the number 261,257 in the place value chart below.

Hundred thousands	Ten Thousands	Thousands	Hundreds	Tens	Ones

Write a number that has the digit 5 in a place that is ten times greater than digit 5 in 261,257.	
Write a number that has the digit 6 in a place that is ten times greater than digit 6 in 261,257.	
Write a number that has the digit 7 in a place that is ten times greater than digit 7 in 261,257.	

2 Write the number 481,079 in the place value chart below.

Hundred thousands	Ten Thousands	Thousands	Hundreds	Tens	Ones

Write a number that has the digit 9 in a place that is ten times greater than digit 9 in 481,079.	
Write a number that has the digit 4 in a place that is ten times greater than digit 4 in 481,079.	
Write a number that has the digit 1 in a place that is ten times greater than digit 1 in 481,079.	

TAKING ON THE B.E.S.T.

 10 Times Less

1 Write the number 100,539 in the place value chart below.

Hundred thousands	Ten Thousands	Thousands	Hundreds	Tens	Ones

Write a number that has the digit 5 in a place that is ten times less than or $\frac{1}{10}$ of digit 5 in 100,539.	
Write a number that has the digit 1 in a place that is ten times less than or $\frac{1}{10}$ of digit 1 in 100,539.	
Write a number that has the digit 3 in a place that is ten times less than or $\frac{1}{10}$ of digit 3 in 100,539.	

2 Write the number 657,809 in the place value chart below.

Hundred thousands	Ten Thousands	Thousands	Hundreds	Tens	Ones

Write a number that has the digit 8 in a place that is $\frac{1}{10}$ of digit 8 in 657,809.	
Write a number that has the digit 6 in a place that is ten times less than the digit 6 in 657,809.	
Write a number that has the digit 7 in a place that is $\frac{1}{10}$ of digit 7 in 657,809.	

26

TAKING ON THE B.E.S.T.

1 Write the number 736,812 in the place value chart below.

Hundred thousands	Ten Thousands	Thousands	Hundreds	Tens	Ones

Write a number that has the digit 1 in a place that is ten times less than the digit 1 in 736,812.	
Write a number that has the digit 7 in a place that is $\frac{1}{10}$ of digit 7 in 736,812.	
Write a number that has the digit 3 in a place that is $\frac{1}{10}$ of digit 3 in 736,812.	

2 Write the number 254,389 in the place value chart below.

Hundred thousands	Ten Thousands	Thousands	Hundreds	Tens	Ones

Write a number that has the digit 2 in a place that is ten times less than the digit 2 in 254,389.	
Write a number that has the digit 8 in a place that is $\frac{1}{10}$ of digit 8 in 254,389.	
Write a number that has the digit 4 in a place that is ten times less than the digit 4 in 254,389.	

27

TAKING ON THE B.E.S.T.

1 Here is the number 19,203. Write a number where the digit 2 is ten times greater than the digit 2 in 19,203.

2 Here is the number 742,680. Write a number where the digit 4 is ten times less than the digit 4 in 742,680.

3 Here is the number 566,941. Write a number where the digit 9 is $\frac{1}{10}$ of the digit 9 in 566,941.

4 Here is the number 67,213. Write a number where the digit 2 is ten times less than the digit 2 in 67,213.

5 Here is the number 399,487. Write a number where the digit 8 is ten times greater than the digit 8 in 399,487.

TAKING ON THE B.E.S.T.

1 Here is the number 743,069. Write a number where the digit 4 is ten times greater than the digit 4 in 743,069.

2 Here is the number 512,008. Write a number where the digit 1 is ten times less than the digit 1 in 512,008.

3 Here is the number 19,289. Write a number where the digit 2 is $\frac{1}{10}$ of the digit 2 in 19,289.

4 Here is the number 400,018. Write a number where the digit 4 is ten times less than the digit 4 in 400,018.

5 Here is the number 16,977. Write a number where the digit 1 is ten times greater than the digit 1 in 16,977.

29

TAKING ON THE B.E.S.T.

PART ONE

Anthony receives a step tracker for his birthday. In July, he realizes that he has logged 243,817 steps.

The next month, he sets a goal to walk further than his steps in July. He also wants to make sure that the value of the 8 in his August goal is ten times greater than the value of the 8 in his July total.

What could be a possible goal for Anthony to reach in August? Explain your thinking.

PART TWO

Anthony's sister, Jasmine, says a possible goal for Anthony to reach in August could be 243,781. Do you agree with Jasmine's number? Why or why not?

TAKING ON THE B.E.S.T.

Math Misconception Mystery (PAGE 1)

BEFORE THE VIDEO: Solve the problem on your own.

> Figure out what the mystery number is using the clues below.
> * This is a 5-digit number.
> * The value of the 4 is 10 times greater than the value of the 4 in 14.
> * The value of the 8 is 10 times less than the value of the 8 in 1,287.
> * The value of the 1 is 10 times greater than the value of the 1 in 641,052.
> * The value of the 3 is $\frac{1}{10}$ of the value of the 3 in 34,201.
> * This missing digit has no value.
>
> What is the mystery number?

DURING THE VIDEO: Pause after each "character" solves the problem and jot down quick notes to help you remember what they did correctly or incorrectly.

Character #1 _____	Character #2 _____
Character #3 _____	**Character #4** _____

31

TAKING ON THE B.E.S.T.

MA.4.NSO.1.1	Math Misconception Mystery (PAGE 2)

AFTER THE VIDEO: Discuss and analyze their answers.

The most reasonable answer belongs to Character # _____ because

_____

_____

_____

_____

(Justify how this character's work makes sense.)

Let's help the others:

	Character #___:	Character #___:	Character #___:
What did this character do that was correct?			
Identify their error			
What do they need to know to understand for next time?			

32

STANDARD FORM	983,256
WORD FORM	
EXPANDED FORM	

STANDARD FORM	
WORD FORM	
EXPANDED FORM	500,000 + 40,000 + 9,000 + 70

33

TAKING ON THE B.E.S.T.

Fill in the blank spaces in the tables below.

1

STANDARD FORM	100,006
WORD FORM	

2

STANDARD FORM	
WORD FORM	four hundred thousand, twenty two

3

STANDARD FORM	115,039
WORD FORM	

4

STANDARD FORM	
WORD FORM	six hundred six thousand, six hundred

5

STANDARD FORM	880,088
WORD FORM	

Fill in the blank spaces in the tables below.

1

STANDARD FORM	813,297
EXPANDED FORM	

2

STANDARD FORM	
EXPANDED FORM	500,000 + 40,000 + 1,000 + 70

3

STANDARD FORM	
EXPANDED FORM	(6 x 100,000) + (2 x 1,000) + (4 x 10) + (5 x 1)

35

TAKING ON THE B.E.S.T.

Fill in the blank spaces in the tables below.

1

STANDARD FORM	
WORD FORM	two hundred sixty-seven thousand, four hundred two
EXPANDED FORM	

2

STANDARD FORM	
WORD FORM	
EXPANDED FORM	
	(5 x 100,000) + (3 x 10,000) + (4 x 10) + (8 x 1)

TAKING ON THE B.E.S.T.

Fill in the blank spaces in the tables below.

1

STANDARD FORM	67,803
WORD FORM	
EXPANDED FORM	

2

STANDARD FORM	
WORD FORM	
EXPANDED FORM	40,000 + 6,000 + 700 + 20 + 1

1 Decompose this number THREE different ways..

213,406		

2 Decompose this number THREE different ways.

710,048		

TAKING ON THE B.E.S.T.

1 Which of the following shows a way to decompose 325,432?
Ⓐ 325 thousands + 43 hundreds + 2 ones
Ⓑ 325 thousands + 4 hundreds + 32 tens
Ⓒ 32 ten thousands + 54 hundreds + 32 tens
Ⓓ 32 ten thousands + 54 hundreds + 32 ones

2 Which of the following shows a way to decompose 711,079?
Ⓐ 71 ten thousands + 10 hundreds + 7 tens + 9 ones
Ⓑ 71 ten thousands + 10 hundreds + 79 tens
Ⓒ 71 ten thousands + 1 thousand + 79 tens
Ⓓ 71 ten thousands + 1 thousand + 7 hundreds + 9 ones

3 Which of the following shows a way to decompose 993,960?
Ⓐ 9 hundred thousands + 93 thousands + 9 hundreds + 60 tens
Ⓑ 9 hundred thousands + 939 hundreds + 60 ones
Ⓒ 99 ten thousands + 396 tens + 60 ones
Ⓓ 99 ten thousands + 396 ones

TAKING ON THE B.E.S.T.

1 Select all of the ways to decompose 112,874.
- Ⓐ 11 ten thousands + 28 hundreds + 74 ones
- Ⓑ 11 ten thousands + 28 thousands + 74 tens
- Ⓒ 1 hundred thousand + 12 thousands + 87 hundreds + 4 tens
- Ⓓ 1 hundred thousand + 12 hundreds + 87 tens + 4 ones
- Ⓔ 112 thousands + 87 tens + 4 ones

2 Select all of the ways to decompose 200,032.
- Ⓐ 2 hundreds + 32 ones
- Ⓑ 2 hundred thousands + 3 tens + 2 ones
- Ⓒ 200 thousands + 32 ones
- Ⓓ 20 ten thousands + 32 tens
- Ⓔ 200 thousands + 32 tens

3 Select all of the ways to decompose 801,456.
- Ⓐ 801 thousands + 45 tens + 6 ones
- Ⓑ 80 ten thousands + 14 hundreds + 56 ones
- Ⓒ 801 hundreds + 45 tens + 6 ones
- Ⓓ 8 hundred thousand + 145 tens + 6 ones
- Ⓔ 80 thousands + 1 hundred + 456 ones

40

1 Decompose this number THREE different ways by regrouping at least one digit.

993,406

2 Decompose this number THREE different ways by regrouping at least one digit.

814,458

MA.4.NSO.1.2 | **Extra Practice #7** | **Decomposing Numbers #2**

---

1 Which of the following shows a way to decompose 316,027?
Ⓐ 30 ten thousands + 16 thousands + 2 hundreds + 7 ones
Ⓑ 30 ten thousands + 16 thousands + 1 ten + 17 ones
Ⓒ 300 thousands + 159 hundreds+ 10 tens + 17 ones
Ⓓ 3 hundred thousands + 16 thousands + 1 hundred + 1 ten + 17 ones

---

2 Which of the following does NOT show a way to decompose 402,243?
Ⓐ 39 ten thousands + 12 thousands + 23 tens + 13 ones
Ⓑ 39 ten thousands + 12 thousands + 24 tens + 3 ones
Ⓒ 390 thousands + 12 thousands + 1 hundred + 43 ones
Ⓓ 390 thousands + 12 thousands + 1 hundred + 143 tens

---

3 Which of the following shows a way to decompose 815,815?
Ⓐ 81 ten thousands + 5 thousands + 18 hundreds + 15 ones
Ⓑ 81 ten thousands + 4 thousands + 18 hundreds + 15 tens
Ⓒ 80 ten thousands + 14 thousands + 18 hundreds + 15 tens
Ⓓ 80 ten thousands + 14 thousands + 18 hundreds + 15 ones

TAKING ON THE B.E.S.T.

1 Select all of the ways to decompose 900,513.
- Ⓐ 890 thousands + 1 thousand + 4 hundreds + 10 tens + 13 ones
- Ⓑ 900 thousands + 14 hundreds + 11 tens + 3 ones
- Ⓒ 890 thousands + 1 ten thousands + 5 hundreds + 1 ten + 3 ones
- Ⓓ 5 hundreds + 11 tens + 3 ones
- Ⓔ 899 thousands + 1 thousand + 5 hundreds + 13 ones

2 Select all of the ways to decompose 13,559.
- Ⓐ 12 thousands + 14 hundreds + 15 tens + 9 ones
- Ⓑ 12 thousands + 14 hundreds + 5 tens + 9 ones
- Ⓒ 1 ten thousand + 34 hundreds + 15 tens + 59 ones
- Ⓓ 13 thousands + 4 hundreds + 15 tens + 9 ones
- Ⓔ 12 thousands + 14 hundreds + 1 ten + 59 ones

3 Select all of the ways to decompose 86,427.
- Ⓐ 85 thousands + 13 hundreds + 11 tens + 17 ones
- Ⓑ 8 ten thousands + 5 thousands + 141 tens + 17 ones
- Ⓒ 85 thousands + 14 hundreds + 27 ones
- Ⓓ 8 ten thousands + 6 thousands + 32 tens + 17 ones
- Ⓔ 86 thousands + 42 hundreds + 7 ones

MA.4.NSO.1.2 | **Math Missions** | **Reading and Writing Numbers**

Use the number 198,203 to complete the following tasks.

PART ONE

Express the number in **word form** and **expanded form**.

PART TWO

Express the number using only **thousands** and **ones**.

PART THREE

Fill in the missing values to correctly decompose the number.

18 ten-thousands + _____ thousands + _____ tens + 13 ones

44

TAKING ON THE B.E.S.T.

Math Misconception Mystery
(PAGE 1)

BEFORE THE VIDEO: Solve the problem on your own.

Which of the following does NOT represent a way to write four hundred six thousand, forty six?

Ⓐ (4 x 100,000) + (6 x 1,000) + (4 x 10) + (6 x 1)
Ⓑ 40 ten thousands + 60 hundreds + 46 ones
Ⓒ 400,000 + 6,000 + 40 + 6
Ⓓ 4 hundred thousands + 60 tens + 46 ones

DURING THE VIDEO: Pause after each "character" solves the problem and jot down quick notes to help you remember what they did correctly or incorrectly.

Character #1 _____

Character #2 _____

Character #3 _____

Character #4 _____

45

TAKING ON THE B.E.S.T.

MA.4.NSO.1.2	Math Misconception Mystery (PAGE 2)

AFTER THE VIDEO: Discuss and analyze their answers.

The most reasonable answer belongs to Character # _____ because

_____

_____

_____

_____

(Justify how this character's work makes sense.)

Let's help the others:

	Character #___:	Character #___:	Character #___:
What did this character do that was correct?			
Identify their error			
What do they need to know to understand for next time?			

46

TAKING ON THE B.E.S.T.

  Video Lesson | Comparing Two Numbers Using Place Value

1 Compare 86,469 and 86,496 using place value.

2 Compare 713,408 and 73,408 using place value.

3 Compare 101,414 and 104,141 using place value.

MA.4.NSO.1.3 | **Extra Practice #1** | **Comparing Two Numbers Using Place Value**

1 Compare 70,344 and 70,433 using place value.

2 Compare 100,234 and 10,235 using place value.

3 Compare 216,384 and 218,391 using place value.

TAKING ON THE B.E.S.T.

1 Compare 15,515 and 15,155 using the number line.

15,100   15,200   15,300   15,400   15,500   15,600

2 Compare 400,281 and 401,302 using the number line below.

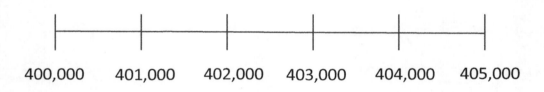

400,000   401,000   402,000   403,000   404,000   405,000

3 Compare 50,084 and 170,840 using the number line below.

0   50,000   100,000   150,000   200,000   250,000   300,000

TAKING ON THE B.E.S.T.

MA.4.NSO.1.3 | **Extra Practice #2** | **Comparing Two Numbers Using a Number Line**

1 Compare 30,744 and 30,747 using the number line.

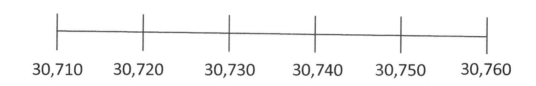

30,710 30,720 30,730 30,740 30,750 30,760

2 Compare 517,192 and 517,291 using the number line below.

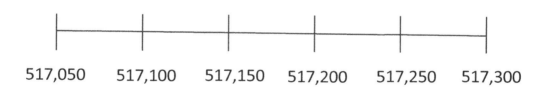

517,050 517,100 517,150 517,200 517,250 517,300

3 Compare 999,099 and 999,909 using the number line below.

998,800 999,000 999,200 999,400 999,600 999,800 1,000,000

© McCarthy Math Academy

TAKING ON THE B.E.S.T.

1 Plot the numbers to order them from LEAST to GREATEST:

25,189; 25,198; 24,981

24,800   24,900   25,000   25,100   25,200   25,300

2 Plot the numbers to order them from LEAST to GREATEST.

601,467; 601,764; 600,674; 600,764

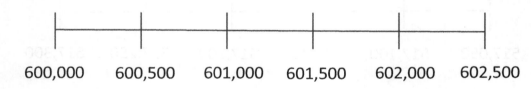

600,000   600,500   601,000   601,500   602,000   602,500

3 Plot the numbers to order them from GREATEST to LEAST.

4,555; 15,454; 9,554; 21,955

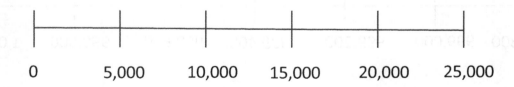

0   5,000   10,000   15,000   20,000   25,000

TAKING ON THE B.E.S.T.

1 Plot the numbers to order them from LEAST to GREATEST:

34,258; 32,548; 32,854

32,000   32,500   33,000   33,500   34,000   34,500

2 Plot the numbers to order them from LEAST to GREATEST.

311,773; 311,737; 311,377

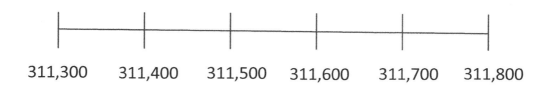

311,300   311,400   311,500   311,600   311,700   311,800

3 Plot the numbers to order them from GREATEST to LEAST.

422,169; 422,196; 421,296; 421,269

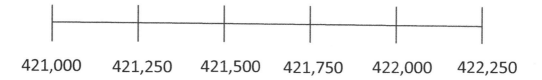

421,000   421,250   421,500   421,750   422,000   422,250

TAKING ON THE B.E.S.T.

MA.4.NSO.I.3	Math Missions	Plot and Order Numbers

PART ONE

Use the cards below to create three different numbers. The digit in the thousands place has been given.

CARDS

3   4   5

4   0   3, ☐ ☐ ☐

4   0   3, ☐ ☐ ☐

4   0   3, ☐ ☐ ☐

PART TWO

Arrange the numbers in ascending order (least to greatest). Use BOTH place value strategies and a number line to explain your thinking.

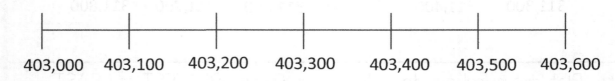

403,000   403,100   403,200   403,300   403,400   403,500   403,600

_____

_____

_____

_____

TAKING ON THE B.E.S.T.

Math Misconception Mystery
(PAGE I)

BEFORE THE VIDEO: Solve the problem on your own.

Use <, >, or = to correctly compare 199,616 and 199,661. Justify your comparison using place value.

DURING THE VIDEO: Pause after each "character" solves the problem and jot down quick notes to help you remember what they did correctly or incorrectly.

Character #1 _____

Character #2 _____

Character #3 _____

Character #4 _____

54

TAKING ON THE B.E.S.T.

Math Misconception Mystery
(PAGE 2)

AFTER THE VIDEO: Discuss and analyze their answers.

The most reasonable answer belongs to Character # _____ because

_____

_____

_____

_____

(Justify how this character's work makes sense.)

Let's help the others:

	Character #___:	Character #___:	Character #___:
What did this character do that was correct?			
Identify their error			
What do they need to know to understand for next time?			

55

TAKING ON THE B.E.S.T.

  **Video Lesson** **Round to the Nearest 10 and 100**

1 Round 3,317 to the nearest ten and hundred. Use a number line and place value strategies to show your thinking.

	Nearest 10	Nearest 100
Number Line		
Place Value Strategies		

2 Round 8,726 to the nearest ten and hundred. Use a number line and place value strategies to show your thinking.

	Nearest 10	Nearest 100
Number Line		
Place Value Strategies		

3 Round 9,534 to the nearest ten and hundred. Use a number line and place value strategies to show your thinking.

	Nearest 10	Nearest 100
Number Line		
Place Value Strategies		

TAKING ON THE B.E.S.T.

1 Round 6,065 to the nearest ten and hundred. Use a number line and place value strategies to show your thinking.

	Nearest 10	Nearest 100
Number Line		
Place Value Strategies		

2 Round 1,803 to the nearest ten and hundred. Use a number line and place value strategies to show your thinking.

	Nearest 10	Nearest 100
Number Line		
Place Value Strategies		

3 Round 8,623to the nearest ten and hundred. Use a number line and place value strategies to show your thinking.

	Nearest 10	Nearest 100
Number Line		
Place Value Strategies		

TAKING ON THE B.E.S.T.

1   Round 7,654 to the nearest ten and thousand. Use a number line and place value strategies to show your thinking.

	Nearest 10	Nearest 1,000
Number Line		
Place Value Strategies		

2   Round 5,257 to the nearest hundred and thousand. Use a number line and place value strategies to show your thinking.

	Nearest 100	Nearest 1,000
Number Line		
Place Value Strategies		

3   Round 9,989 to the nearest ten, hundred, and thousand. Use a number line and place value strategies to show your thinking.

	Nearest 10	Nearest 100	Nearest 1,000
Number Line			
Place Value Strategies			

TAKING ON THE B.E.S.T.

1 Round 5,450 to the nearest ten and thousand. Use a number line and place value strategies to show your thinking.

	Nearest 10	Nearest 1,000
Number Line		
Place Value Strategies		

2 Round 8,823 to the nearest hundred and thousand. Use a number line and place value strategies to show your thinking.

	Nearest 100	Nearest 1,000
Number Line		
Place Value Strategies		

3 Round 4,162 to the nearest ten, hundred, and thousand. Use a number line and place value strategies to show your thinking.

	Nearest 10	Nearest 100	Nearest 1,000
Number Line			
Place Value Strategies			

TAKING ON THE B.E.S.T.

1 Round 4,014 to the nearest ten and hundred. Use a number line and place value strategies to show your thinking.

	Nearest 10	Nearest 100
Number Line		
Place Value Strategies		

2 Round 6,998 to the nearest thousand and ten. Use a number line and place value strategies to show your thinking.

	Nearest 1,000	Nearest 10
Number Line		
Place Value Strategies		

3 Round 1,230 to the nearest ten, hundred, and thousand. Use a number line and place value strategies to show your thinking.

	Nearest 10	Nearest 100	Nearest 1,000
Number Line			
Place Value Strategies			

60

TAKING ON THE B.E.S.T.

MA.4.NSO.1.4  Video Lesson | **Estimating Sums and Differences**

1 Use rounding to estimate the sum of 6,234 and 3,171.

2 Use rounding to estimate the difference of 9,982 from 4,713.

3 Use rounding to estimate the sum of 4,828 and 512. Then, estimate the difference of 512 from 4,828.

61

TAKING ON THE B.E.S.T.

1 Use rounding to estimate the sum of 7,469 and 1,471.

2 Use rounding to estimate the difference of 6,890 from 3,017.

3 Use rounding to estimate the sum of 9,765 and 999. Then, estimate the difference of 999 from 9,765.

TAKING ON THE B.E.S.T.

MA.4.NSO.1.4	Math Mission	Rounding to the Nearest 10, 100, and 1,000

PART ONE

Use the cards below to create three different numbers. Then, round the numbers that you create to the nearest ten, hundred, thousand.

CARDS

4	7	2	5

Round to the Nearest 10	Round to the Nearest 100	Round to the Nearest 1,000

PART TWO

Tosha creates a number using the same cards. Her number rounded to the nearest hundred is 2,500. What is the number that Tosha creates from the cards? Explain your thinking.

_____

_____

_____

_____

TAKING ON THE B.E.S.T.

BEFORE THE VIDEO: Solve the problem on your own.

Ava has $7,283 in her savings account. Round this amount to the nearest ten, hundred, and thousand.

DURING THE VIDEO: Pause after each "character" solves the problem and jot down quick notes to help you remember what they did correctly or incorrectly.

Character #1 _____

Character #2 _____

Character #3 _____

Character #4 _____

TAKING ON THE B.E.S.T.

MA.4.NSO.1.4 | Math Misconception Mystery (PAGE 2)

AFTER THE VIDEO: Discuss and analyze their answers.

The most reasonable answer belongs to Character # _____ because

_____

_____

_____

(Justify how this character's work makes sense.)

Let's help the others:

	Character #___:	Character #___:	Character #___:
What did this character do that was correct?			
Identify their error			
What do they need to know to understand for next time?			

TAKING ON THE B.E.S.T.

1 Model each decimal number using the area models below. Then, order them from LEAST to GREATEST. Finally, complete the comparison statements with the correct symbol.

0.34; 0.3; 0.38

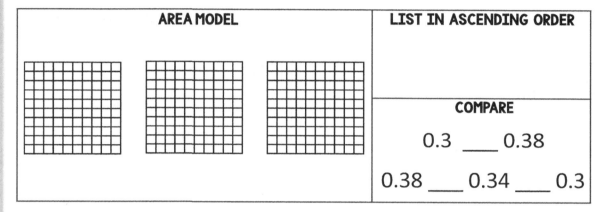

AREA MODEL	LIST IN ASCENDING ORDER
	COMPARE
	0.3 ____ 0.38
	0.38 ____ 0.34 ____ 0.3

2 Model each decimal number using the area models below. Then, order them from LEAST to GREATEST. Finally, complete the comparison statements with the correct symbol.

0.7; 0.07; 0.75

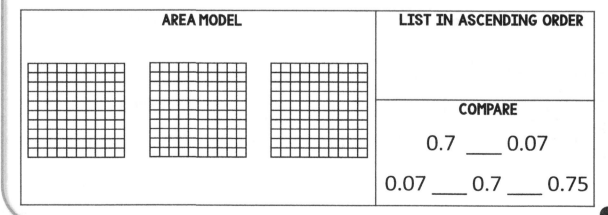

AREA MODEL	LIST IN ASCENDING ORDER
	COMPARE
	0.7 ____ 0.07
	0.07 ____ 0.7 ____ 0.75

66

TAKING ON THE B.E.S.T.

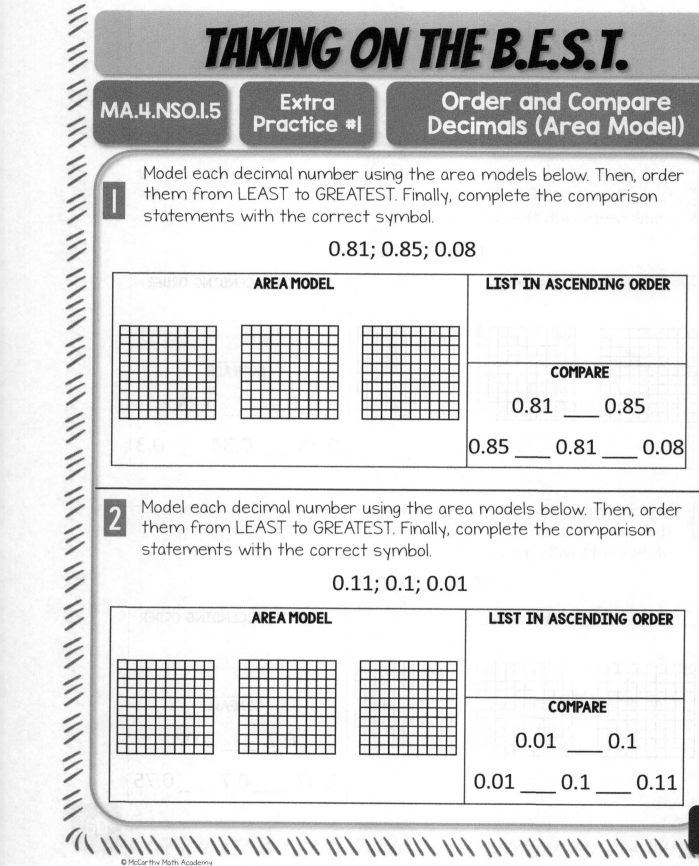

1 Model each decimal number using the area models below. Then, order them from LEAST to GREATEST. Finally, complete the comparison statements with the correct symbol.

0.81; 0.85; 0.08

AREA MODEL	LIST IN ASCENDING ORDER
	COMPARE
	0.81 ____ 0.85
	0.85 ____ 0.81 ____ 0.08

2 Model each decimal number using the area models below. Then, order them from LEAST to GREATEST. Finally, complete the comparison statements with the correct symbol.

0.11; 0.1; 0.01

AREA MODEL	LIST IN ASCENDING ORDER
	COMPARE
	0.01 ____ 0.1
	0.01 ____ 0.1 ____ 0.11

TAKING ON THE B.E.S.T.

1 Model each decimal number using the area models below. Then, order them from LEAST to GREATEST. Finally, complete the comparison statements with the correct symbol.

0.66; 0.06; 0.6

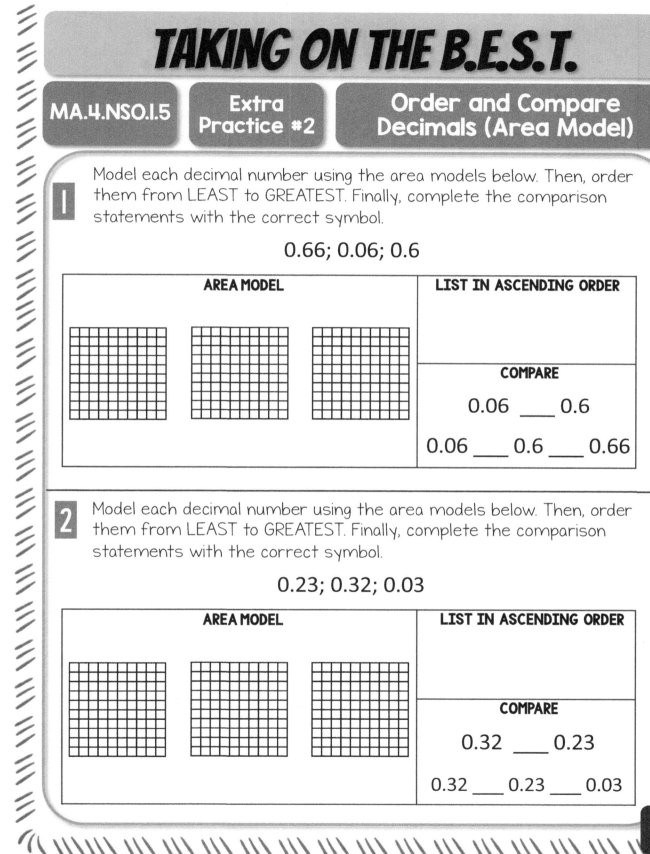

AREA MODEL	LIST IN ASCENDING ORDER
	COMPARE
	0.06 ___ 0.6
	0.06 ___ 0.6 ___ 0.66

2 Model each decimal number using the area models below. Then, order them from LEAST to GREATEST. Finally, complete the comparison statements with the correct symbol.

0.23; 0.32; 0.03

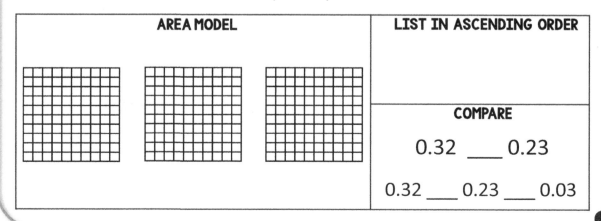

AREA MODEL	LIST IN ASCENDING ORDER
	COMPARE
	0.32 ___ 0.23
	0.32 ___ 0.23 ___ 0.03

TAKING ON THE B.E.S.T.

  **Video Lesson** **Plot, Order, and Compare Decimals (Number Line)**

1 Plot each decimal number using the number line below. Then, order them from LEAST to GREATEST. Finally, complete the comparison statements with the correct symbol.

2.56; 2.47; 2.5

NUMBER LINE	LIST IN ASCENDING ORDER
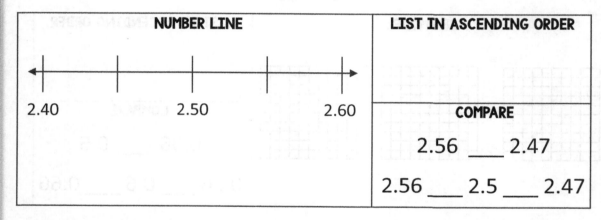 2.40 2.50 2.60	
	COMPARE
	2.56 ___ 2.47
	2.56 ___ 2.5 ___ 2.47

2 Plot each decimal number using the number line below. Then, order them from LEAST to GREATEST. Finally, complete the comparison statements with the correct symbol.

7.7; 7.67; 7.76

NUMBER LINE	LIST IN ASCENDING ORDER
7.5 7.6 7.7 7.8 7.9	
	COMPARE
	7.67 ___ 7.76
	7.67 ___ 7.7 ___ 7.76

69

TAKING ON THE B.E.S.T.

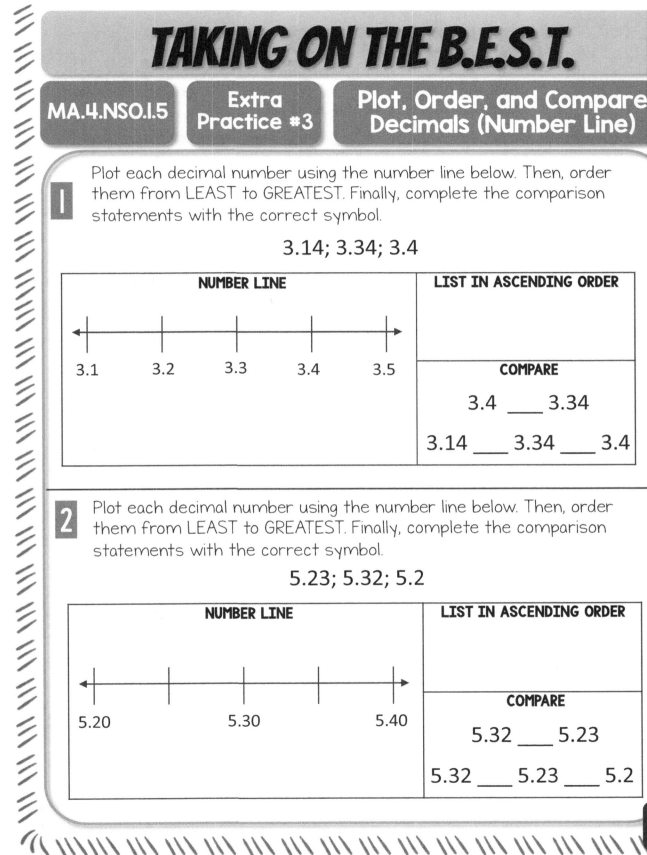

1 Plot each decimal number using the number line below. Then, order them from LEAST to GREATEST. Finally, complete the comparison statements with the correct symbol.

3.14; 3.34; 3.4

NUMBER LINE	LIST IN ASCENDING ORDER

3.1   3.2   3.3   3.4   3.5

COMPARE
3.4 ___ 3.34
3.14 ___ 3.34 ___ 3.4

2 Plot each decimal number using the number line below. Then, order them from LEAST to GREATEST. Finally, complete the comparison statements with the correct symbol.

5.23; 5.32; 5.2

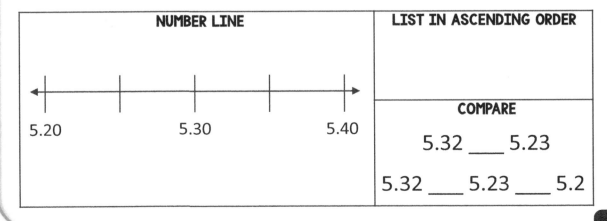

NUMBER LINE	LIST IN ASCENDING ORDER

5.20   5.30   5.40

COMPARE
5.32 ___ 5.23
5.32 ___ 5.23 ___ 5.2

70

TAKING ON THE B.E.S.T.

| **Extra Practice #4** | **Plot, Order, and Compare Decimals (Number Line)**

1 Plot each decimal number using the number line below. Then, order them from LEAST to GREATEST. Finally, complete the comparison statements with the correct symbol.

9.44; 9.4; 9.5

NUMBER LINE	LIST IN ASCENDING ORDER

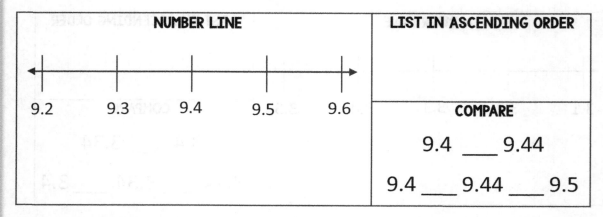

9.2   9.3   9.4   9.5   9.6

COMPARE
9.4 ___ 9.44
9.4 ___ 9.44 ___ 9.5

2 Plot each decimal number using the number line below. Then, order them from LEAST to GREATEST. Finally, complete the comparison statements with the correct symbol.

1.0; 1.01; 1.11

NUMBER LINE	LIST IN ASCENDING ORDER

1.0   1.1   1.2

COMPARE
1.0 ___ 1.01
1.11 ___ 1.01 ___ 1.0

TAKING ON THE B.E.S.T.

MA.4.NSO.1.5 | **Math Missions** | **Plot, Order, and Compare Decimals**

Four students in Mrs. Thompson's class share how many hours they have volunteered this month. Nikkem has completed 4.05 hours, and Raul has completed 4.15 hours. Klaudia has completed 4.5 hours, and Todrick has completed 4.45 hours.

PART ONE

Plot and label the students' times on the number line below.

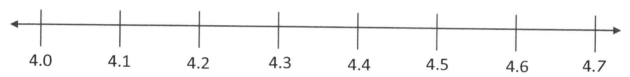

4.0   4.1   4.2   4.3   4.4   4.5   4.6   4.7

TIME SPENT VOLUNTEERING (IN HOURS)

PART TWO

List their times in order from LEAST to GREATEST (ascending order).

[   ] ; [   ] ; [   ] ; [   ]

List their times in order from GREATEST TO LEAST (descending order).

[   ] ; [   ] ; [   ] ; [   ]

PART THREE:

Todrick says that he has completed more volunteer hours than Nikkem, Raul, and Klaudia. Explain Todrick's error.

_____

_____

_____

TAKING ON THE B.E.S.T.

Math Misconception Mystery (PAGE 1)

BEFORE THE VIDEO: Solve the problem on your own.

Select all the values that would make the following comparison a true statement.

$$1.3 < \underline{\qquad}$$

Ⓐ 1.03
Ⓑ 1.30
Ⓒ 1.33
Ⓓ 0.33
Ⓔ 13.0

DURING THE VIDEO: Pause after each "character" solves the problem and jot down quick notes to help you remember what they did correctly or incorrectly.

Character #1 _____	Character #2 _____
Character #3 _____	Character #4 _____

TAKING ON THE B.E.S.T.

Math Misconception Mystery (PAGE 2)

AFTER THE VIDEO: Discuss and analyze their answers.

The most reasonable answer belongs to Character # _____ because

_____

_____

_____

_____

(Justify how this character's work makes sense.)

Let's help the others:

	Character #___:	Character #___:	Character #___:
What did this character do that was correct?			
Identify their error			
What do they need to know to understand for next time?			

74

TAKING ON THE B.E.S.T.

  Video Lesson | **Multiplication and Division Facts (Basic Strategies)**

1   6 x 8

SKIP COUNTING	FACT FAMILY

2   4 x 6

SKIP COUNTING	FACT FAMILY

3   7 x 3

SKIP COUNTING	FACT FAMILY

75

| MA.4.NSO.2.1 | Extra Practice #1 | Multiplication and Division Facts (Basic Strategies) |

1   7 x 6

SKIP COUNTING	FACT FAMILY

2   4 x 8

SKIP COUNTING	FACT FAMILY

3   9 x 5

SKIP COUNTING	FACT FAMILY

76

TAKING ON THE B.E.S.T.

1   **0**

6 x 0 = _____

0 x 8 = _____

2   **1**

6 x 1 = _____

1 x 8 = _____

12 ÷ 1 = _____

3   **5**

4 x 5 = _____

5 x 8 = _____

55 ÷ 5 = _____

4   **10**

10 x 3 = _____

7 x 10 = _____

120 ÷ 10 = _____

77

TAKING ON THE B.E.S.T.

1   0

$12 \times 0 = \_\_\_\_$

$0 \times 3 = \_\_\_\_$

2   1

$12 \times 1 = \_\_\_\_$

$1 \times 3 = \_\_\_\_$

$11 \div 1 = \_\_\_\_$

3   5

$3 \times 5 = \_\_\_\_$

$5 \times 9 = \_\_\_\_$

$60 \div 5 = \_\_\_\_$

4   10

$10 \times 4 = \_\_\_\_$

$11 \times 10 = \_\_\_\_$

$90 \div 10 = \_\_\_\_$

78

TAKING ON THE B.E.S.T.

 Video Lesson

Multiplication and Division Facts (2s, 4s, 8s)

1 **2**

2 x 2 = _____

4 x 2 = _____

14 ÷ 2 = _____

2 **4**

4 x 3 = _____

4 x 7 = _____

40 ÷ 4 = _____

3 **8**

8 x 5 = _____

3 x 8 = _____

8 x 11 = _____

79

TAKING ON THE B.E.S.T.

1   **2**

2 x 3 = _____

6 x 2 = _____

24 ÷ 2 = _____

2   **4**

4 x 6 = _____

4 x 8 = _____

12 x 4 = _____

3   **8**

8 x 6 = _____

9 x 8 = _____

8 x 12 = _____

TAKING ON THE B.E.S.T.

1   6 x 8 = _____

2   7 x 6 = _____

3   12 x 8 = _____

3   11 x 11 = _____

TAKING ON THE B.E.S.T.

Extra Practice #4 **Distributive Property of Multiplication**

1   7 x 7 = _____

2   8 x 8 = _____

3   12 x 4 = _____

3   11 x 7 = _____

MA.4.NSO.2.1 | **Extra Practice #5** | **Distributive Property of Multiplication**

1   9 x 12 = _____

2   6 x 6 = _____

3   12 x 7 = _____

3   11 x 12 = _____

TAKING ON THE B.E.S.T.

MA.4.NSO.2.1 | **Math Missions** | **Multiplication and Division Facts**

PART ONE

Explain how you can quickly recall multiplication facts with a factor of 0.

_____

_____

_____

_____

PART TWO

Explain how you can quickly recall multiplication facts with a factor of 1.

_____

_____

_____

_____

PART THREE

Explain how the 5s facts and 10 facts for multiplication are related.

_____

_____

_____

_____

TAKING ON THE B.E.S.T.

MA.4.NSO.2.1

Math Misconception Mystery
(PAGE 1)

BEFORE THE VIDEO: Solve the problem on your own.

Select all the equations that have 4 as a the missing value.

(A) $24 \div 4 = ?$
(B) $11 \times ? = 44$
(C) $8 \times ? = 12$
(D) $48 \div 8 = ?$
(E) $? \times 9 = 36$

DURING THE VIDEO: Pause after each "character" solves the problem and jot down quick notes to help you remember what they did correctly or incorrectly.

Character #1 _____	Character #2 _____
Character #3 _____	**Character #4** _____

85

© McCarthy Math Academy

TAKING ON THE B.E.S.T.

MA.4.NSO.2.1 **Math Misconception Mystery (PAGE 2)**

AFTER THE VIDEO: Discuss and analyze their answers.

The most reasonable answer belongs to Character # _____ because

_____

_____

_____

_____

(Justify how this character's work makes sense.)

Let's help the others:

	Character #___:	Character #___:	Character #___:
What did this character do that was correct?			
Identify their error			
What do they need to know to understand for next time?			

86

TAKING ON THE B.E.S.T.

1 26 x 8   ESTIMATE:

AREA MODEL	PARTIAL PRODUCTS

2 53 x 3   ESTIMATE:

AREA MODEL	PARTIAL PRODUCTS

TAKING ON THE B.E.S.T.

1 51 x 7   ESTIMATE:

AREA MODEL	PARTIAL PRODUCTS

2 46 x 6   ESTIMATE:

AREA MODEL	PARTIAL PRODUCTS

TAKING ON THE B.E.S.T.

 Video Lesson

Multiply Whole Numbers
2 Digits x 2 Digits

1 34 x 29 ESTIMATE:

AREA MODEL	PARTIAL PRODUCTS

2 65 x 18 ESTIMATE:

AREA MODEL	PARTIAL PRODUCTS

MA.4.NSO.2.2 | **Extra Practice #2** | **Multiply Whole Numbers 2 Digits x 2 Digits**

1 88 x 23 | ESTIMATE:

AREA MODEL	PARTIAL PRODUCTS

2 32 x 56 | ESTIMATE:

AREA MODEL	PARTIAL PRODUCTS

TAKING ON THE B.E.S.T.

1   304 x 67   ESTIMATE:

AREA MODEL	PARTIAL PRODUCTS

2   122 x 92   ESTIMATE:

AREA MODEL	PARTIAL PRODUCTS

91

TAKING ON THE B.E.S.T.

1   412 x 49   **ESTIMATE:**

AREA MODEL	PARTIAL PRODUCTS

2   876 x 27   **ESTIMATE:**

AREA MODEL	PARTIAL PRODUCTS

TAKING ON THE B.E.S.T.

MA.4.NSO.2.2	Extra Practice #4	Multiply Whole Numbers 3 Digits x 2 Digits

1   728 x 11   **ESTIMATE:**

AREA MODEL

PARTIAL PRODUCTS

2   408 x 15   **ESTIMATE:**

AREA MODEL

PARTIAL PRODUCTS

93

© McCarthy Math Academy

TAKING ON THE B.E.S.T.

Michelle earns $15 for every lawn she mows.

PART ONE

How much money will Michelle earn if she mows 7 lawns?

PART TWO

How much money will Michelle earn if she mows 48 lawns?

PART THREE

Michelle is saving up her money to buy a new laptop. The laptops costs $1,499. Michelle sets a goal to mow 105 lawns. Will she have enough money to purchase the new laptop? Explain your reasoning.

_____

_____

_____

_____

MA.4.NSO.2.2 | Math Misconception Mystery (PAGE 1)

BEFORE THE VIDEO: Solve the problem on your own.

> What is the product of 149 and 63?

DURING THE VIDEO: Pause after each "character" solves the problem and jot down quick notes to help you remember what they did correctly or incorrectly.

Character #1 _____

Character #2 _____

Character #3 _____

Character #4 _____

TAKING ON THE B.E.S.T.

MA.4.NSO.2.2 | ## Math Misconception Mystery
(PAGE 2)

AFTER THE VIDEO: Discuss and analyze their answers.

The most reasonable answer belongs to Character # _____ because
_____
_____
_____
_____
(Justify how this character's work makes sense.)

Let's help the others:

	Character #___:	Character #___:	Character #___:
What did this character do that was correct?			
Identify their error			
What do they need to know to understand for next time?			

96

TAKING ON THE B.E.S.T.

1 36 x 7   ESTIMATE:

STANDARD ALGORITHM

2 52 x 8   ESTIMATE:

STANDARD ALGORITHM

TAKING ON THE B.E.S.T.

1   81 x 3   **ESTIMATE:**

STANDARD ALGORITHM

2   76 x 2   **ESTIMATE:**

STANDARD ALGORITHM

TAKING ON THE B.E.S.T.

1 66 x 7   ESTIMATE:

STANDARD ALGORITHM

2 42 x 4   ESTIMATE:

STANDARD ALGORITHM

TAKING ON THE B.E.S.T.

1 73 x 18   **ESTIMATE:**

STANDARD ALGORITHM

2 46 x 32   **ESTIMATE:**

STANDARD ALGORITHM

100

TAKING ON THE B.E.S.T.

1 22 x 41   ESTIMATE:

STANDARD ALGORITHM

2 26 x 59   ESTIMATE:

STANDARD ALGORITHM

101

1   21 x 62   **ESTIMATE:**

STANDARD ALGORITHM

2   99 x 34   **ESTIMATE:**

STANDARD ALGORITHM

TAKING ON THE B.E.S.T.

MA.4.NSO.2.3	Math Missions	Multiply Whole Numbers

PART ONE

Use each card one time to create two 2-digit numbers that when multiplied, will have a product greater than 2,600.

CARDS

$$\boxed{1} \quad \boxed{3} \quad \boxed{2} \quad \boxed{9}$$

PART TWO

Finn says it is impossible to use the same cards to create two 2-digit numbers that, when multiplied, contain a product less than 500. Explain how Finn's theory is incorrect.

_____

_____

_____

_____

TAKING ON THE B.E.S.T.

MA.4.NSO.2.3

Math Misconception Mystery
(PAGE 1)

BEFORE THE VIDEO: Solve the problem on your own.

What is the product of 24 and 69?

DURING THE VIDEO: Pause after each "character" solves the problem and jot down quick notes to help you remember what they did correctly or incorrectly.

Character #1 _____

Character #2 _____

Character #3 _____

Character #4 _____

MA.4.NSO.2.3 | **Math Misconception Mystery (PAGE 2)**

AFTER THE VIDEO: Discuss and analyze their answers.

The most reasonable answer belongs to Character # _____ because

_____

_____

_____

_____

(Justify how this character's work makes sense.)

Let's help the others:

	Character #___:	Character #___:	Character #___:
What did this character do that was correct?			
Identify their error			
What do they need to know to understand for next time?			

105

TAKING ON THE B.E.S.T.

  Video Lesson | **Divide Up to 4-Digits By 1-Digit (Area Model)**

1 $367 \div 3$ ESTIMATE:

AREA MODEL	CHECK USING MULTIPLICATION

2 $1,284 \div 6$ ESTIMATE:

AREA MODEL	CHECK USING MULTIPLICATION

106

MA.4.NSO.2.4 | **Extra Practice #1** | **Divide Up to 4-Digits By 1-Digit (Area Model)**

1 4,037 ÷ 3 | ESTIMATE:

AREA MODEL	CHECK USING MULTIPLICATION

2 2,855 ÷ 6 | ESTIMATE:

AREA MODEL	CHECK USING MULTIPLICATION

TAKING ON THE B.E.S.T.

Extra Practice #2 **Divide Up to 4-Digits By 1-Digit (Area Model)**

1 $4,037 \div 6$ ESTIMATE:

AREA MODEL	CHECK USING MULTIPLICATION

2 $2,855 \div 2$ ESTIMATE:

AREA MODEL	CHECK USING MULTIPLICATION

TAKING ON THE B.E.S.T.

1 8,702 ÷ 4 | **ESTIMATE:**

PARTIAL QUOTIENTS	CHECK USING MULTIPLICATION

2 3,113 ÷ 5 | **ESTIMATE:**

PARTIAL QUOTIENTS	CHECK USING MULTIPLICATION

109

MA.4.NSO.2.4	Extra Practice #3	Divide Up to 4-Digits By 1-Digit (Partial Quotients)

1   8,702 ÷ 9 | **ESTIMATE:**

PARTIAL QUOTIENTS	CHECK USING MULTIPLICATION

2   3,113 ÷ 2 | **ESTIMATE:**

PARTIAL QUOTIENTS	CHECK USING MULTIPLICATION

110

TAKING ON THE B.E.S.T.

1 $3,087 \div 4$ | ESTIMATE:

PARTIAL QUOTIENTS

CHECK USING MULTIPLICATION

2 $6,009 \div 6$ | ESTIMATE:

PARTIAL QUOTIENTS

CHECK USING MULTIPLICATION

111

© McCarthy Math Academy

TAKING ON THE B.E.S.T.

  Video Lesson | Divide Up to 4-Digits By 1-Digit (Long Division Algorithm)

1 3,702 ÷ 8 | **ESTIMATE:**

LONG DIVISION ALGORITHM | CHECK USING MULTIPLICATION

2 2,177 ÷ 7 | **ESTIMATE:**

LONG DIVISION ALGORITHM | CHECK USING MULTIPLICATION

112

TAKING ON THE B.E.S.T.

MA.4.NSO.2.4 | **Extra Practice #5** | **Divide Up to 4-Digits By 1-Digit (Long Division Algorithm)**

1 3,702 ÷ 7   ESTIMATE:

LONG DIVISION ALGORITHM	CHECK USING MULTIPLICATION

2 2,177 ÷ 2   ESTIMATE:

LONG DIVISION ALGORITHM	CHECK USING MULTIPLICATION

TAKING ON THE B.E.S.T.

1 $5,554 \div 2$ ESTIMATE:

LONG DIVISION ALGORITHM	CHECK USING MULTIPLICATION

2 $309 \div 4$ ESTIMATE:

LONG DIVISION ALGORITHM	CHECK USING MULTIPLICATION

TAKING ON THE B.E.S.T.

MA.4.NSO.2.4	Math Missions	Divide Up to 4-Digits By 1-Digit

PART ONE

Use each card one time to create a division problem that has a quotient of more than 4,000. Show how you can find the exact quotient.

CARDS

☐ ☐ ☐ ☐ ÷ ☐

PART TWO

Francesca says that 6,923 divided by 4 will provide a quotient of more than 2,000. Explain how her theory is incorrect.

_____

_____

_____

_____

115

© McCarthy Math Academy

BEFORE THE VIDEO: Solve the problem on your own.

Find the quotient of 4,098 divided by 4.

DURING THE VIDEO: Pause after each "character" solves the problem and jot down quick notes to help you remember what they did correctly or incorrectly.

Character #1 _____

Character #2 _____

Character #3 _____

Character #4 _____

TAKING ON THE B.E.S.T.

MA.4.NSO.2.4 | Math Misconception Mystery (PAGE 2)

AFTER THE VIDEO: Discuss and analyze their answers.

The most reasonable answer belongs to Character # _____ because

_____

_____

_____

_____

(Justify how this character's work makes sense.)

Let's help the others:

	Character #___:	Character #___:	Character #___:
What did this character do that was correct?			
Identify their error			
What do they need to know to understand for next time?			

117

TAKING ON THE B.E.S.T.

  **Video Lesson** | **Using Estimation to Multiply**

1 Is 21,000 a good estimate for the product of 57 x 323? Explain.

2 Is 35,000 a good estimate for the product of 742 x 38? Explain.

3 Is 8,000 a good estimate for the product of 98 x 82?

118

© McCarthy Math Academy

TAKING ON THE B.E.S.T.

1 Is 16,000 a good estimate for the product of 21 x 816? Explain.

2 Is 3,000 a good estimate for the product of 154 x 21? Explain.

3 Is 54,000 a good estimate for the product of 495 x 89? Explain.

TAKING ON THE B.E.S.T.

1 Is 200 a good estimate for the quotient of 1,523 ÷ 32? Explain.

2 Is 90 a good estimate for the quotient of 7,387 ÷ 83? Explain.

3 Is 300 a good estimate for the quotient of 934 ÷ 31? Explain.

TAKING ON THE B.E.S.T.

1 Is 40 a good estimate for the quotient of 2,644 ÷ 44? Explain.

2 Is 400 a good estimate for the quotient of 4,865 ÷ 12? Explain.

3 Is 80 a good estimate for the quotient of 1,188 ÷ 31? Explain.

TAKING ON THE B.E.S.T.

Mr. Toddy purchased 70 packs of pencils for his students. Each package contains 10 pencils. He wants to give an equal number of pencils to each of his 21 students.

PART ONE

One student estimated that each student in Mr. Toddy's class would get 20 pencils. Do you think this is a good estimate? Why or why not?

_____

_____

_____

_____

PART TWO

Use estimation to determine about how many pencils each student will get. Explain your reasoning.

_____

_____

_____

_____

TAKING ON THE B.E.S.T.

Math Misconception Mystery
(PAGE 1)

BEFORE THE VIDEO: Solve the problem on your own.

> Use estimation to find the product of 73 and 389.

DURING THE VIDEO: Pause after each "character" solves the problem and jot down quick notes to help you remember what they did correctly or incorrectly.

Character #1 _____

Character #2 _____

Character #3 _____

Character #4 _____

TAKING ON THE B.E.S.T.

AFTER THE VIDEO: Discuss and analyze their answers.

The most reasonable answer belongs to Character # _____ because

_____

_____

_____

_____

(Justify how this character's work makes sense.)

Let's help the others:

	Character #___:	Character #___:	Character #___:
What did this character do that was correct?			
Identify their error			
What do they need to know to understand for next time?			

124

TAKING ON THE B.E.S.T.

  Video Lesson **Foundational Skills**

PLACE VALUE

2   .   3   8

VALUE OF DIGITS

2   .   3   8

MODEL WITH BASE TEN BLOCKS

Ones	Tenths	Hundredths

125

TAKING ON THE B.E.S.T.

  Video Lesson | One-Tenth More or Less

1 Write the number 28.15 in the place value chart below.

Tens	Ones	Tenths	Hundredths

Write 28.15 in word form.	
What is **one-tenth more** than 28.15?	
What is **one-tenth less** than 28.15?	

2 Write the number 19.43 in the place value chart below.

Tens	Ones	Tenths	Hundredths

Write 19.43 in word form.	
What is **one-tenth more** than 19.43?	
What is **one-tenth less** than 19.43?	

126

TAKING ON THE B.E.S.T.

1 Write the number 3.24 in the place value chart below.

Tens	Ones	Tenths	Hundredths

Write 3.24 in word form.	
What is **one-tenth more** than 3.24?	
What is **one-tenth less** than 3.24?	

2 Write the number 42.02 in the place value chart below.

Tens	Ones	Tenths	Hundredths

Write 42.02 in word form.	
What is **one-tenth more** than 42.02?	
What is **one-tenth less** than 42.02?	

127

TAKING ON THE B.E.S.T.

1. Write the number 37.86 in the place value chart below.

Tens	Ones	Tenths	Hundredths

Write 37.86 in word form.	
What is **one-tenth more** than 37.86?	
What is **one-tenth less** than 37.86?	

2. Write the number 21.43 in the place value chart below.

Tens	Ones	Tenths	Hundredths

Write 21.43 in word form.	
What is **one-tenth more** than 21.43?	
What is **one-tenth less** than 21.43?	

TAKING ON THE B.E.S.T.

  Video Lesson | One-Hundredth More or Less

1 Write the number 18.45 in the place value chart below.

Tens	Ones	Tenths	Hundredths

Write 18.45 in word form.	
What is **one-hundredth more** than 18.45?	
What is **one-hundredth less** than 18.45?	

2 Write the number 22.31 in the place value chart below.

Tens	Ones	Tenths	Hundredths

Write 22.31 in word form.	
What is **one-hundredth more** than 22.31?	
What is **one-hundredth less** than 22.31?	

129

TAKING ON THE B.E.S.T.

1 Write the number 8.09 in the place value chart below.

Tens	Ones	Tenths	Hundredths

Write 8.09 in word form.	
What is **one-hundredth more** than 8.09?	
What is **one-hundredth less** than 8.09?	

2 Write the number 11.86 in the place value chart below.

Tens	Ones	Tenths	Hundredths

Write 11.86 in word form.	
What is **one-hundredth more** than 11.86?	
What is **one-hundredth less** than 11.86?	

130

TAKING ON THE B.E.S.T.

1 Write the number 75.17 in the place value chart below.

Tens	Ones	Tenths	Hundredths

Write 75.17 in word form.	
What is **one–hundredth more** than 75.17?	
What is **one–hundredth less** than 75.17?	

2 Write the number 30.82 in the place value chart below.

Tens	Ones	Tenths	Hundredths

Write 30.82 in word form.	
What is **one–hundredth more** than 30.82?	
What is **one–hundredth less** than 30.82?	

131

© McCarthy Math Academy

TAKING ON THE B.E.S.T.

MA.4.NSO.2.6 | **Math Missions** | **One-Tenth & One-Hundredth More or Less**

PART ONE

Meisha is thinking of a number. She has included some clues about her number.

Clues:
- My number has 32 tens.
- My number has 4 ones.
- The digit in the tenths place is one-tenth less than 0.8.
- The digit in the hundredths place is one-hundredth more than 0.02.

What is Meisha's number? Explain your reasoning.

_____

_____

_____

_____

PART TWO

Write Meisha's number in word form.

_____

PART THREE

Create a new number that is one-hundredth less than Meisha's number.

_____

TAKING ON THE B.E.S.T.

MA.4.NSO.2.6 | Math Misconception Mystery (PAGE 1)

BEFORE THE VIDEO: Solve the problem on your own.

> What is one-hundredth less than 1.9?

DURING THE VIDEO: Pause after each "character" solves the problem and jot down quick notes to help you remember what they did correctly or incorrectly.

Character #1 _____	Character #2 _____
Character #3 _____	Character #4 _____

133

TAKING ON THE B.E.S.T.

MA.4.NSO.2.6 | **Math Misconception Mystery (PAGE 2)**

AFTER THE VIDEO: Discuss and analyze their answers.

The most reasonable answer belongs to Character # _____ because

_____

_____

_____

_____

(Justify how this character's work makes sense.)

Let's help the others:

	Character #___:	Character #___:	Character #___:
What did this character do that was correct?			
Identify their error			
What do they need to know to understand for next time?			

TAKING ON THE B.E.S.T.

  Video Lesson | **Addition with Decimals: Base-Ten Blocks**

Estimate the sum. Model each expression with base–ten blocks. Then model with a drawing.

 1   3.12 + 0.89   **ESTIMATE:**

2   1.65 + 2.47   **ESTIMATE:**

TAKING ON THE B.E.S.T.

Extra Practice #1

Addition with Decimals: Base-Ten Blocks

Estimate the sum. Model each expression with base-ten blocks. Then model with a drawing.

1 1.33 + 1.92   ESTIMATE:

2 2.25 + 0.76   ESTIMATE:

TAKING ON THE B.E.S.T.

 Video Lesson

Addition with Decimals: Money

Estimate the sum. Model each expression with money. Then draw the bills and coins you used.

1 $3.37 + $0.91   **ESTIMATE:**

2 $4.19 + $1.48   **ESTIMATE:**

137

TAKING ON THE B.E.S.T.

| MA.4.NSO.2.7 | Extra Practice #2 | Addition with Decimals: Money |

Estimate the sum. Model each expression with money. Then draw the bills and coins you used.

1  $2.40 + $0.75   ESTIMATE:

2 $0.35 + $1.86   ESTIMATE:

TAKING ON THE B.E.S.T.

  Video Lesson | **Addition with Decimals: Standard Algorithm**

Estimate the sum. Then use a standard algorithm (based on place value) to solve.

1 20.72 + 2.02   ESTIMATE:

2 16.88 + 3.99   ESTIMATE:

TAKING ON THE B.E.S.T.

| MA.4.NSO.2.7 | Extra Practice #3 | Addition with Decimals: Standard Algorithm |

Estimate the sum. Then use a standard algorithm (based on place value) to solve.

1 18.39 + 5.21   ESTIMATE:

2 1.01 + 5.97   ESTIMATE:

TAKING ON THE B.E.S.T.

Estimate the difference. Model each expression with base-ten blocks. Then model with a drawing.

1   3.12 − 0.89   **ESTIMATE:**

2   2.65 − 1.47   **ESTIMATE:**

TAKING ON THE B.E.S.T.

Extra Practice #4 **Subtraction with Decimals: Base-Ten Blocks**

Estimate the difference. Model each expression with base–ten blocks. Then model with a drawing.

1 2.33 – 1.92   ESTIMATE:

2 2.25 – 0.76   ESTIMATE:

142

TAKING ON THE B.E.S.T.

Estimate the difference. Model each expression with money. Then draw the bills and coins you used.

1 $3.37 – $0.91 | **ESTIMATE:** |

2 $4.19 – $1.48 | **ESTIMATE:** |

143

© McCarthy Math Academy

TAKING ON THE B.E.S.T.

| **Extra Practice #5** | **Subtraction with Decimals: Money**

Estimate the difference. Model each expression with money. Then draw the bills and coins you used.

1 $2.40 – $0.75   ESTIMATE:

2 $4.35 – $1.86   ESTIMATE:

144

TAKING ON THE B.E.S.T.

  Video Lesson | **Subtraction with Decimals: Standard Algorithm**

Estimate the difference. Then use a standard algorithm (based on place value) to solve.

1 20.72 – 2.02   **ESTIMATE:**

2 16.88 – 3.99   **ESTIMATE:**

TAKING ON THE B.E.S.T.

Estimate the difference. Then use a standard algorithm (based on place value) to solve.

1 18.39 – 5.21 | **ESTIMATE:** |

2 7.01 – 5.97 | **ESTIMATE:** |

TAKING ON THE B.E.S.T.

MA.4.NSO.2.7 | **Math Missions** | **Adding & Subtracting Numbers with Decimals**

PART ONE

Marc has $5.31 in his wallet. He wants to purchase glitter pencils for $1.99. He estimates that he will have $2.00 left. Is his estimate reasonable?

_____

_____

_____

_____

PART TWO

How much change will Marc receive after he purchases the glitter pencils?

PART THREE

A few days after purchasing the glitter pencils, Marc receives $7.78 for completing his chores. How much money does he have now?

TAKING ON THE B.E.S.T.

Math Misconception Mystery (PAGE 1)

BEFORE THE VIDEO: Solve the problem on your own.

Estimate, then solve: 4.01 - 2.99

DURING THE VIDEO: Pause after each "character" solves the problem and jot down quick notes to help you remember what they did correctly or incorrectly.

Character #1 _____

Character #2 _____

Character #3 _____

Character #4 _____

148

TAKING ON THE B.E.S.T.

Math Misconception Mystery
(PAGE 2)

AFTER THE VIDEO: Discuss and analyze their answers.

The most reasonable answer belongs to Character # _____ because

_____

_____

_____

_____

(Justify how this character's work makes sense.)

Let's help the others:

	Character #___:	Character #___:	Character #___:
What did this character do that was correct?			
Identify their error			
What do they need to know to understand for next time?			

149

TAKING ON THE B.E.S.T.

Shade the models to complete the equivalent fractions.

1

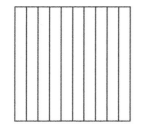

$$\frac{4}{10} = \frac{\boxed{}}{100}$$

3

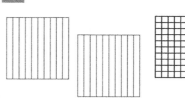

$$\frac{\boxed{}}{10} = \frac{120}{100}$$

2

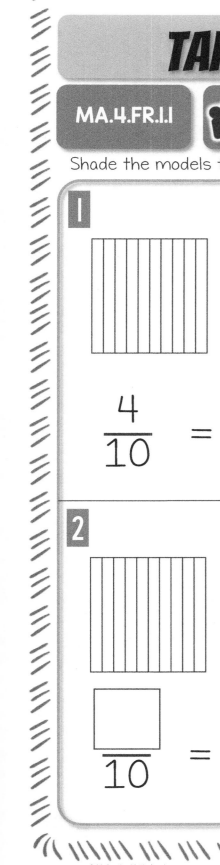

$$\frac{\boxed{}}{10} = \frac{70}{100}$$

4

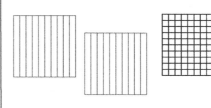

$$\frac{14}{10} = \frac{\boxed{}}{100}$$

150

© McCarthy Math Academy

TAKING ON THE B.E.S.T.

MA.4.FR.1.1	Extra Practice #1	Equivalent Fractions with Denominators of 10 and 100 (Area Model)

Shade the models to complete the equivalent fractions.

1

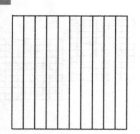 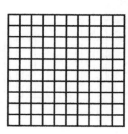

$$\frac{5}{10} = \frac{\boxed{}}{100}$$

3

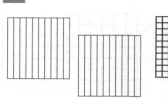 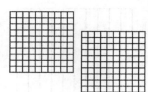

$$\frac{\boxed{}}{10} = \frac{110}{100}$$

2

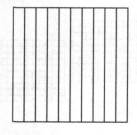 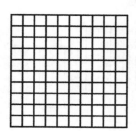

$$\frac{\boxed{}}{10} = \frac{90}{100}$$

4

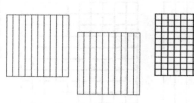 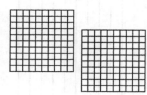

$$\frac{17}{10} = \frac{\boxed{}}{100}$$

151

TAKING ON THE B.E.S.T.

Plot the points of each fraction to determine the equivalent fraction.

1

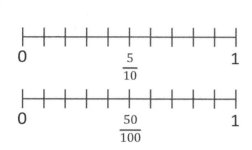

$$\frac{3}{10} = \frac{}{100}$$

3

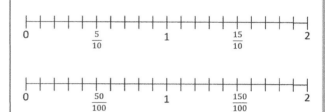

$$\frac{}{10} = \frac{200}{100}$$

2

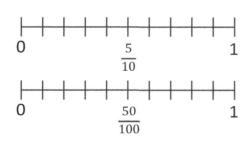

$$\frac{}{10} = \frac{80}{100}$$

4

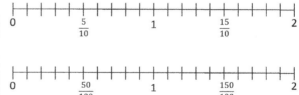

$$\frac{13}{10} = \frac{}{100}$$

152

TAKING ON THE B.E.S.T.

Plot the points of each fraction to determine the equivalent fraction.

1

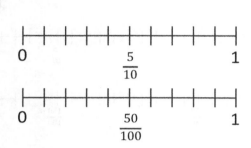

$$\frac{1}{10} = \frac{\boxed{}}{100}$$

2

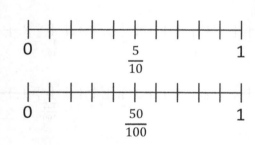

$$\frac{\boxed{}}{10} = \frac{60}{100}$$

3

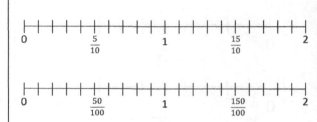

$$\frac{\boxed{}}{10} = \frac{190}{100}$$

4

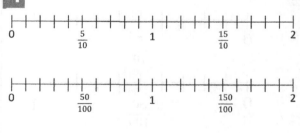

$$\frac{18}{10} = \frac{\boxed{}}{100}$$

153

TAKING ON THE B.E.S.T.

PART ONE

A fraction is modeled below. Write the fraction that is represented.

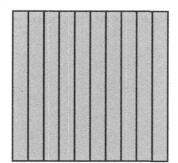 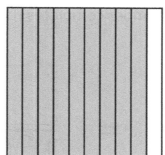 

PART TWO

Write an equivalent fraction to the one above that has a denominator of 100. Then model this fraction on the area model below.

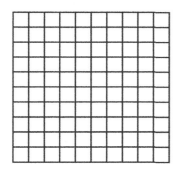 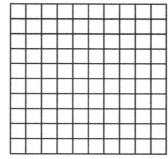 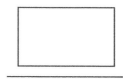

100

PART THREE

Plot the two fractions on the number lines below to justify that they are equivalent.

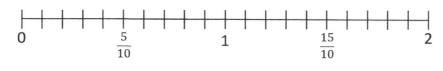

TAKING ON THE B.E.S.T.

| MA.4.FR.1.1 | Math Misconception Mystery (PAGE I) |

BEFORE THE VIDEO: Solve the problem on your own.

An equation is shown. What number completes the equivalent fraction?

$$\frac{7}{10} = \frac{\square}{100}$$

DURING THE VIDEO: Pause after each "character" solves the problem and jot down quick notes to help you remember what they did correctly or incorrectly.

Character #1 _____

Character #2 _____

Character #3 _____

Character #4 _____

155

TAKING ON THE B.E.S.T.

Math Misconception Mystery (PAGE 2)

AFTER THE VIDEO: Discuss and analyze their answers.

The most reasonable answer belongs to Character # _____ because

_____

_____

_____

_____

(Justify how this character's work makes sense.)

Let's help the others:

	Character #___:	Character #___:	Character #___:
What did this character do that was correct?			
Identify their error			
What do they need to know to understand for next time?			

156

TAKING ON THE B.E.S.T.

Model the fractions by shading in the value of the fraction. Then, write the values in decimal form.

1

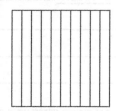

$$\frac{4}{10} = \boxed{}$$

What other names represent this fraction?

3

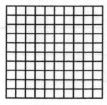

$$\frac{5}{100} = \boxed{}$$

What other names represent this fraction?

2

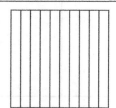

$$\frac{5}{10} = \boxed{}$$

What other names represent this fraction?

4

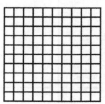

$$\frac{29}{100} = \boxed{}$$

What other names represent this fraction?

TAKING ON THE B.E.S.T.

Model the fractions by shading in the value of the fraction. Then, write the values in decimal form.

1

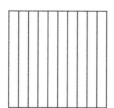

$\frac{6}{10}$ = ⬚

What other names represent this fraction?

3

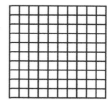

$\frac{48}{100}$ = ⬚

What other names represent this fraction?

2

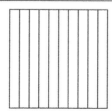

$\frac{7}{10}$ = ⬚

What other names represent this fraction?

4

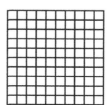

$\frac{12}{100}$ = ⬚

What other names represent this fraction?

158

TAKING ON THE B.E.S.T.

Plot the fractions on the number lines. Then, write the values in decimal form.

1

0   1

$\frac{3}{10}$ = [ ]

What other names represent this fraction?

3

0   1

$\frac{75}{100}$ = [ ]

What other names represent this fraction?

2

0   1

$\frac{9}{10}$ = [ ]

What other names represent this fraction?

4

0   1

$\frac{31}{100}$ = [ ]

What other names represent this fraction?

159

MA.4.FR.I.2 | **Extra Practice #2** | **Relate Fractions and Decimals Less Than One** (Number Line)

Plot the fractions on the number lines. Then, write the values in decimal form.

1

0   1

$\dfrac{8}{10}$ = [ ]

What other names represent this fraction?

3

0   1

$\dfrac{58}{100}$ = [ ]

What other names represent this fraction?

2

0   1

$\dfrac{1}{10}$ = [ ]

What other names represent this fraction?

4

0   1

$\dfrac{82}{100}$ = [ ]

What other names represent this fraction?

160

TAKING ON THE B.E.S.T.

Model the fractions by shading in the value of the fraction. Then, write the values in decimal form.

1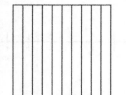

$$\frac{15}{10} = \boxed{}$$

What other names represent this fraction?

3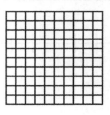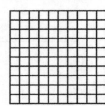

$$\frac{155}{100} = \boxed{}$$

What other names represent this fraction?

2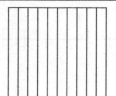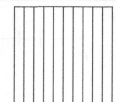

$$\frac{20}{10} = \boxed{}$$

What other names represent this fraction?

4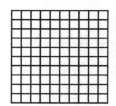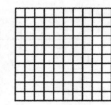

$$\frac{147}{100} = \boxed{}$$

What other names represent this fraction?

161

TAKING ON THE B.E.S.T.

Model the fractions by shading in the value of the fraction. Then, write the values in decimal form.

1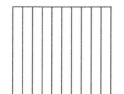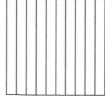

$$\frac{14}{10} = \boxed{}$$

What other names represent this fraction?

3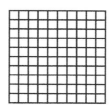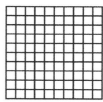

$$\frac{123}{100} = \boxed{}$$

What other names represent this fraction?

2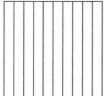

$$\frac{19}{10} = \boxed{}$$

What other names represent this fraction?

4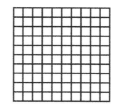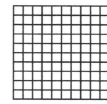

$$\frac{160}{100} = \boxed{}$$

What other names represent this fraction?

TAKING ON THE B.E.S.T.

   Video Lesson **Relate Fractions and Decimals Greater Than One** (Number Line)

Plot the fractions on the number lines. Then, write the values in decimal form.

1

0 ——————— 1 ——————— 2 ——————— 3

$$\frac{21}{10} = \boxed{}$$

What other names represent this fraction?

3

0 ——————— 1 ——————— 2 ——————— 3

$$\frac{132}{100} = \boxed{}$$

What other names represent this fraction?

2

0 ——————— 1 ——————— 2 ——————— 3

$$\frac{13}{10} = \boxed{}$$

What other names represent this fraction?

4

0 ——————— 1 ——————— 2 ——————— 3

$$\frac{149}{100} = \boxed{}$$

What other names represent this fraction?

163

MA.4.FR.I.2 | **Extra Practice #4** | **Relate Fractions and Decimals Greater Than One** (Number Line)

Plot the fractions on the number lines. Then, write the values in decimal form.

1

$$\frac{18}{10} = \boxed{}$$

What other names represent this fraction?

3

$$\frac{137}{100} = \boxed{}$$

What other names represent this fraction?

2

$$\frac{28}{10} = \boxed{}$$

What other names represent this fraction?

4

$$\frac{294}{100} = \boxed{}$$

What other names represent this fraction?

164

TAKING ON THE B.E.S.T.

MA.4.FR.I.2 | **Math Missions** | **Relate Fractions and Decimals**

PART ONE

Model the decimal number **1.2** on the area model below.

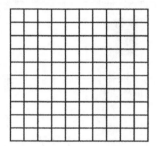 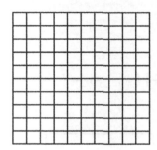

PART TWO

Rewrite **1.2** as four different fractions or mixed numbers.

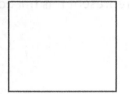   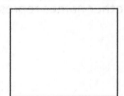

PART THREE

Jermica plots **1.2** on the number line below. She explains, "For **1.2**, you must plot the point halfway between the 1 and the 2."

Explain Jermica's mistake on the lines below. Then, plot the point correctly on the number line.

_____

_____

_____

_____

165

| MA.4.FR.1.2 | Math Misconception Mystery (PAGE 1) |

BEFORE THE VIDEO: Solve the problem on your own.

Express the fraction as a decimal.

$$\frac{4}{100} = \boxed{}$$

DURING THE VIDEO: Pause after each "character" solves the problem and jot down quick notes to help you remember what they did correctly or incorrectly.

Character #1 _____	Character #2 _____
Character #3 _____	Character #4 _____

TAKING ON THE B.E.S.T.

Math Misconception Mystery
(PAGE 2)

AFTER THE VIDEO: Discuss and analyze their answers.

The most reasonable answer belongs to Character # _____ because

_____

_____

_____

_____

(Justify how this character's work makes sense.)

Let's help the others:

	Character #___:	Character #___:	Character #___:
What did this character do that was correct?			
Identify their error			
What do they need to know to understand for next time?			

167

TAKING ON THE B.E.S.T.

1 Determine if $\frac{3}{5}$ and $\frac{6}{10}$ are equivalent by drawing area models.

If the fractions are equivalent, describe how numerator and denominator are affected.

2 Determine if $\frac{3}{8}$ and $\frac{2}{4}$ are equivalent by drawing area models.

If the fractions are equivalent, describe how numerator and denominator are affected.

3 Determine if $\frac{1}{3}$ and $\frac{2}{6}$ are equivalent by drawing area models.

If the fractions are equivalent, describe how numerator and denominator are affected.

168

© McCarthy Math Academy

TAKING ON THE B.E.S.T.

1 Determine if $\frac{2}{3}$ and $\frac{4}{8}$ are equivalent by drawing area models.

If the fractions are equivalent, describe how numerator and denominator are affected.

2 Determine if $\frac{2}{2}$ and $\frac{6}{6}$ are equivalent by drawing area models.

If the fractions are equivalent, describe how numerator and denominator are affected.

3 Determine if $\frac{9}{12}$ and $\frac{3}{4}$ are equivalent by drawing area models.

If the fractions are equivalent, describe how numerator and denominator are affected.

169

TAKING ON THE B.E.S.T.

|  Video Lesson | **Equivalent Fractions (Number Lines)**

1 Determine if $\frac{3}{4}$ and $\frac{6}{8}$ are equivalent using the number lines below.

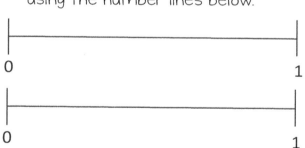

0   1

0   1

If the fractions are equivalent, describe how numerator and denominator are affected.

2 Determine if $\frac{1}{2}$ and $\frac{1}{3}$ are equivalent using the number lines below.

0   1

0   1

If the fractions are equivalent, describe how numerator and denominator are affected.

3 Determine if $\frac{1}{2}$ and $\frac{5}{10}$ are equivalent using the number lines below.

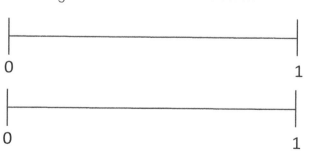

0   1

0   1

If the fractions are equivalent, describe how numerator and denominator are affected.

TAKING ON THE B.E.S.T.

1 Determine if $\frac{2}{4}$ and $\frac{5}{8}$ are equivalent using the number lines below.

0 ———————————— 1

0 ———————————— 1

If the fractions are equivalent, describe how numerator and denominator are affected.

2 Determine if $\frac{5}{6}$ and $\frac{10}{12}$ are equivalent using the number lines below.

0 ———————————— 1

0 ———————————— 1

If the fractions are equivalent, describe how numerator and denominator are affected.

3 Determine if $\frac{1}{2}$ and $\frac{4}{6}$ are equivalent using the number lines below.

0 ———————————— 1

0 ———————————— 1

If the fractions are equivalent, describe how numerator and denominator are affected.

171

TAKING ON THE B.E.S.T.

  **Video Lesson** **Equivalent Fractions (Sets)**

1 Determine if $\frac{3}{5}$ and $\frac{6}{10}$ are equivalent by creating sets.

If the fractions are equivalent, describe how numerator and denominator are affected.

2 Determine if $\frac{2}{3}$ and $\frac{6}{10}$ are equivalent by creating sets.

If the fractions are equivalent, describe how numerator and denominator are affected.

3 Determine if $\frac{1}{4}$ and $\frac{3}{12}$ are equivalent by creating sets.

If the fractions are equivalent, describe how numerator and denominator are affected.

TAKING ON THE B.E.S.T.

1 Determine if $\frac{4}{5}$ and $\frac{9}{10}$ are equivalent by creating sets.

If the fractions are equivalent, describe how numerator and denominator are affected.

2 Determine if $\frac{1}{3}$ and $\frac{4}{12}$ are equivalent by creating sets.

If the fractions are equivalent, describe how numerator and denominator are affected.

3 Determine if $\frac{1}{4}$ and $\frac{2}{10}$ are equivalent by creating sets.

If the fractions are equivalent, describe how numerator and denominator are affected.

1   Determine if $1\frac{2}{10}$ and $1\frac{4}{5}$ are equivalent by drawing area models and using the number lines below.


```
0           1           2
|-----------|-----------|

0           1           2
|-----------|-----------|
```

If the fractions are equivalent, describe how numerator and denominator are affected.

2   Determine if $\frac{3}{2}$ and $\frac{6}{4}$ are equivalent by drawing area models and using the number lines below.

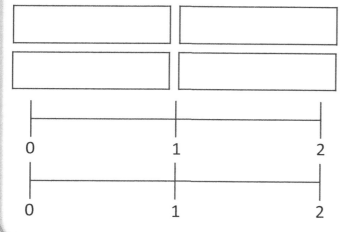

If the fractions are equivalent, describe how numerator and denominator are affected.

174

TAKING ON THE B.E.S.T.

MA.4.FR.1.3 | **Extra Practice #4** | **Equivalent Fractions (Fractions Greater Than One)**

---

1 Determine if $1\frac{1}{3}$ and $1\frac{2}{5}$ are equivalent by drawing area models and using the number lines below.

If the fractions are equivalent, describe how numerator and denominator are affected.

0   1   2

0   1   2

---

2 Determine if $\frac{6}{5}$ and $\frac{9}{8}$ are equivalent by drawing area models and using the number lines below.

If the fractions are equivalent, describe how numerator and denominator are affected.

0   1   2

0   1   2

175

© McCarthy Math Academy

TAKING ON THE B.E.S.T.

MA.4.FR.1.3 | **Math Missions** | **Equivalent Fractions**

PART ONE

Use the cards to create three equivalent fractions.

CARDS

1	2	3	4	5
6	8	10	12	

PART TWO

Model or prove how you know these three fractions are equivalent at least three different ways.

176

TAKING ON THE B.E.S.T.

Math Misconception Mystery
(PAGE I)

BEFORE THE VIDEO: Solve the problem on your own.

Create a fraction that is equivalent to the fraction below.

$$\frac{9}{6} = \boxed{}$$

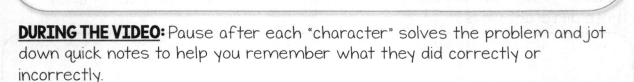

DURING THE VIDEO: Pause after each "character" solves the problem and jot down quick notes to help you remember what they did correctly or incorrectly.

Character #1 _____

Character #2 _____

Character #3 _____

Character #4 _____

TAKING ON THE B.E.S.T.

Math Misconception Mystery (PAGE 2)

AFTER THE VIDEO: Discuss and analyze their answers.

The most reasonable answer belongs to Character # _____ because

_____

_____

_____

_____

(Justify how this character's work makes sense.)

Let's help the others:

	Character #___:	Character #___:	Character #___:
What did this character do that was correct?			
Identify their error			
What do they need to know to understand for next time?			

178

TAKING ON THE B.E.S.T.

Use benchmark fractions to compare the fractions using the symbols <, >, or = .

1

$\frac{2}{3}$ ◯ $\frac{1}{4}$

0 —— $\frac{1}{4}$ —— $\frac{1}{2}$ —— $\frac{3}{4}$ —— 1

Justify your comparison in words.

2

$\frac{3}{8}$ ◯ $\frac{5}{6}$

0 —— $\frac{1}{4}$ —— $\frac{1}{2}$ —— $\frac{3}{4}$ —— 1

Justify your comparison in words.

3

$\frac{3}{5}$ ◯ $\frac{1}{3}$

0 —— $\frac{1}{4}$ —— $\frac{1}{2}$ —— $\frac{3}{4}$ —— 1

Justify your comparison in words.

TAKING ON THE B.E.S.T.

MA.4.FR.I.4 | **Extra Practice #1** | **Using Benchmark Fractions**

Use benchmark fractions to compare the fractions using the symbols <, >, or = .

1

$\frac{8}{12}$ ◯ $\frac{2}{6}$

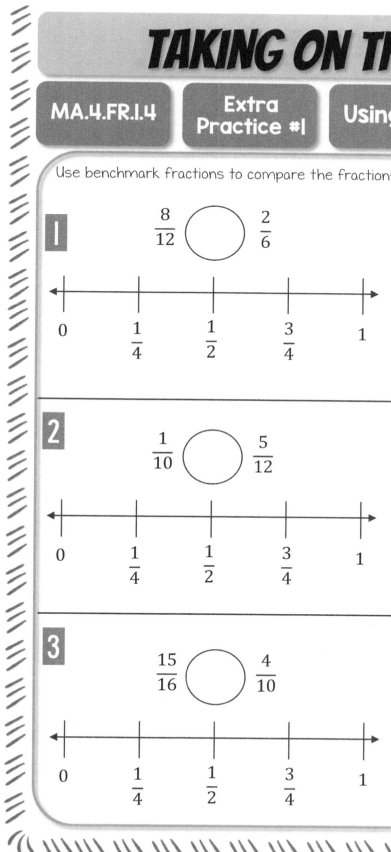

0    $\frac{1}{4}$ $\frac{1}{2}$ $\frac{3}{4}$ 1

Justify your comparison in words.

2

$\frac{1}{10}$ ◯ $\frac{5}{12}$

0    $\frac{1}{4}$ $\frac{1}{2}$ $\frac{3}{4}$ 1

Justify your comparison in words.

3

$\frac{15}{16}$ ◯ $\frac{4}{10}$

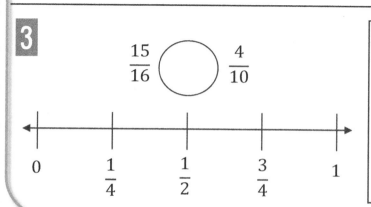

0    $\frac{1}{4}$ $\frac{1}{2}$ $\frac{3}{4}$ 1

Justify your comparison in words.

180

TAKING ON THE B.E.S.T.

  Video Lesson | Plot, Order, and Compare Fractions Less Than One

1 Plot each fraction using the number line below. Then, order them from LEAST to GREATEST. Finally, complete the comparison statements with the correct symbol.

$$\frac{3}{10}, \frac{1}{8}, \frac{4}{16}$$

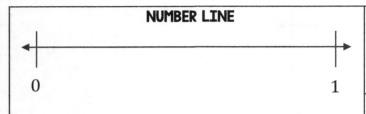

NUMBER LINE	LIST IN ASCENDING ORDER
0 ———— 1	

COMPARE

$$\frac{4}{16} \underline{\quad} \frac{3}{10}$$

$$\frac{1}{8} \underline{\quad} \frac{4}{16} \underline{\quad} \frac{3}{10}$$

2 Plot each fraction using the number line below. Then, order them from GREATEST to LEAST. Finally, complete the comparison statements with the correct symbol

$$\frac{7}{12}, \frac{7}{10}, \frac{7}{8}$$

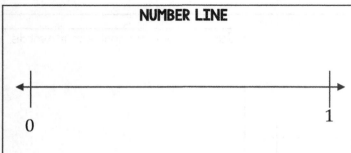

NUMBER LINE	LIST IN DESCENDING ORDER
0 ———— 1	

COMPARE

$$\frac{7}{12} \underline{\quad} \frac{7}{8}$$

$$\frac{7}{8} \underline{\quad} \frac{7}{10} \underline{\quad} \frac{7}{12}$$

TAKING ON THE B.E.S.T.

MA.4.FR.1.4	Extra Practice #2	Plot, Order, and Compare Fractions Less Than One

1 Plot each fraction using the number line below. Then, order them from LEAST to GREATEST. Finally, complete the comparison statements with the correct symbol.

$$\frac{1}{4}, \frac{3}{6}, \frac{1}{16}$$

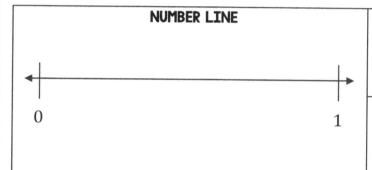

NUMBER LINE	LIST IN ASCENDING ORDER
0 ——————— 1	
	COMPARE
	$\frac{1}{4}$ —— $\frac{1}{16}$
	$\frac{3}{6}$ —— $\frac{1}{4}$ —— $\frac{1}{16}$

2 Plot each fraction using the number line below. Then, order them from GREATEST to LEAST. Finally, complete the comparison statements with the correct symbol

$$\frac{1}{2}, \frac{3}{5}, \frac{5}{12}$$

NUMBER LINE	LIST IN DESCENDING ORDER
0 ——————— 1	
	COMPARE
	$\frac{5}{12}$ —— $\frac{3}{5}$
	$\frac{5}{12}$ —— $\frac{1}{2}$ —— $\frac{3}{5}$

182

© McCarthy Math Academy

TAKING ON THE B.E.S.T.

1 Plot each fraction using the number line below. Then, order them from GREATEST to LEAST. Finally, complete the comparison statements with the correct symbol.

$$2\frac{11}{12}, \; 2\frac{2}{16}, \; 1\frac{5}{10}$$

NUMBER LINE	LIST IN DESCENDING ORDER
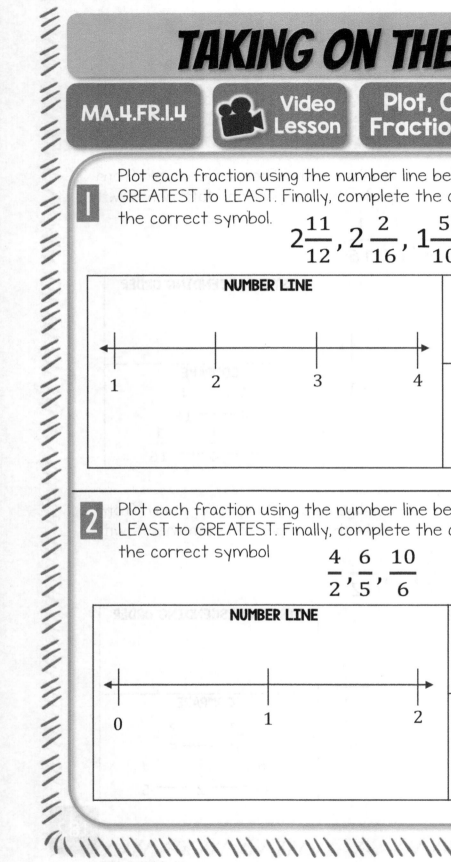 1 2 3 4	
	COMPARE
	$2\frac{2}{16}$ ——— $2\frac{11}{12}$

2 Plot each fraction using the number line below. Then, order them from LEAST to GREATEST. Finally, complete the comparison statements with the correct symbol

$$\frac{4}{2}, \; \frac{6}{5}, \; \frac{10}{6}$$

NUMBER LINE	LIST IN ASCENDING ORDER
0 1 2	
	COMPARE
	$\frac{4}{2}$ ——— $\frac{10}{6}$

183

TAKING ON THE B.E.S.T.

1 Plot each fraction using the number line below. Then, order them from GREATEST to LEAST. Finally, complete the comparison statements with the correct symbol.

$$3\frac{3}{8}, \ 2\frac{6}{10}, \ 3\frac{8}{12}$$

NUMBER LINE	LIST IN DESCENDING ORDER

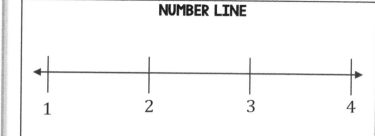

Number line labeled 1, 2, 3, 4

COMPARE

$$3\frac{3}{8} \underline{\quad\quad} 3\frac{8}{12}$$

2 Plot each fraction using the number line below. Then, order them from LEAST to GREATEST. Finally, complete the comparison statements with the correct symbol

$$\frac{7}{4}, \ \frac{8}{3}, \ \frac{10}{8}$$

NUMBER LINE	LIST IN ASCENDING ORDER

Number line labeled 1, 2, 3

COMPARE

$$\frac{8}{3} \underline{\quad\quad} \frac{10}{8}$$

184

TAKING ON THE B.E.S.T.

| MA.4.FR.1.4 | Math Missions | Plot, Order, and Compare Fractions |

Camari tracks his running distances over the course of the week in the table below.

DAY OF WEEK	DISTANCE (IN MILES)
Monday	$3\frac{2}{5}$
Wednesday	$2\frac{9}{10}$
Thursday	$\frac{21}{6}$
Friday	$1\frac{10}{12}$
Sunday	$\frac{16}{4}$

PART ONE
Plot Camari's running distances on the number line below.

$$\longleftrightarrow$$

PART TWO
Which day did he run the furthest distance? _____

Which day did he run the shortest distance? _____

PART THREE
The following week, Camari wants to run even farther than his greatest distance. What would be a possible goal for him to set?

_____

_____

_____

TAKING ON THE B.E.S.T.

| **Math Misconception Mystery (PAGE 1)**

BEFORE THE VIDEO: Solve the problem on your own.

Plot the fractions on the number line. Then, order the fractions from GREATEST to LEAST.

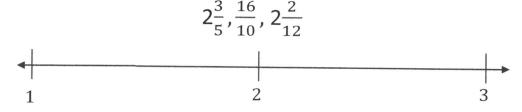

$$2\frac{3}{5}, \frac{16}{10}, 2\frac{2}{12}$$

1   2   3

DURING THE VIDEO: Pause after each "character" solves the problem and jot down quick notes to help you remember what they did correctly or incorrectly.

Character #1 _____	Character #2 _____
Character #3 _____	Character #4 _____

186

TAKING ON THE B.E.S.T.

Math Misconception Mystery
(PAGE 2)

AFTER THE VIDEO: Discuss and analyze their answers.

The most reasonable answer belongs to Character # _____ because

_____

_____

_____

_____

(Justify how this character's work makes sense.)

Let's help the others:

	Character #___:	Character #___:	Character #___:
What did this character do that was correct?			
Identify their error			
What do they need to know to understand for next time?			

187

TAKING ON THE B.E.S.T.

  **Video Lesson** | **Decompose Fractions into a Sum of Fractions** (Fractions Less Than One)

Decompose each fraction two different ways. Include a visual fraction model, and write an equation to show how you decomposed each fraction.

1 $\dfrac{5}{8}$ | $\dfrac{5}{8}$

2 $\dfrac{9}{10}$ | $\dfrac{9}{10}$

3 $\dfrac{11}{16}$ | $\dfrac{11}{16}$

TAKING ON THE B.E.S.T.

Extra Practice #1

Decompose Fractions into a Sum of Fractions
(Fractions Less Than One)

Decompose each fraction two different ways. Include a visual fraction model, and write an equation to show how you decomposed each fraction.

1 $\dfrac{3}{4}$ $\qquad\qquad\qquad\qquad$ $\dfrac{3}{4}$

2 $\dfrac{7}{8}$ $\qquad\qquad\qquad\qquad$ $\dfrac{7}{8}$

3 $\dfrac{10}{12}$ $\qquad\qquad\qquad\qquad$ $\dfrac{10}{12}$

MA.4.FR.2.1

 **Video Lesson**

Decompose Fractions into a Sum of Fractions
(Fractions Greater Than One)

Decompose each fraction two different ways. Include a visual fraction model, and write an equation to show how you decomposed each fraction.

1 $2\dfrac{3}{12}$ $2\dfrac{3}{12}$

2 $\dfrac{9}{5}$ $\dfrac{9}{5}$

3 $\dfrac{10}{3}$ $\dfrac{10}{3}$

TAKING ON THE B.E.S.T.

Extra Practice #2

Decompose Fractions into a Sum of Fractions
(Fractions Greater Than One)

Decompose each fraction two different ways. Include a visual fraction model, and write an equation to show how you decomposed each fraction.

1

$1\frac{7}{10}$

$1\frac{7}{10}$

2

$\frac{11}{4}$

$\frac{11}{4}$

3

$\frac{12}{6}$

$\frac{12}{6}$

TAKING ON THE B.E.S.T.

| MA.4.FR.2.1 | Math Missions | Decompose Fractions into a Sum of Fractions |

Ethan ordered pizza for his family. He ordered 4 boxes of pizza, with each pizza divided into eighths.

PART ONE

Provide a visual fraction model of the pizza below. Label each pizza as a sum of fractions.

PART TWO

The visual model below shows the amount of pizza remaining after Ethan's family eats. Each shaded portion represents a pizza slice. Label each pizza as a sum of fractions.

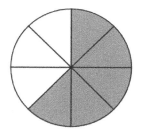 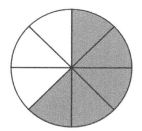 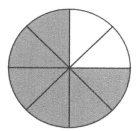 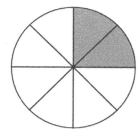

PART THREE

How can you represent the remaining pizza slices as a sum of fractions a different way? Model with an equation.

TAKING ON THE B.E.S.T.

MA.4.FR.2.1 | Math Misconception Mystery (PAGE 1)

BEFORE THE VIDEO: Solve the problem on your own.

Select all that represent a sum to express $\frac{11}{4}$.

Ⓐ $\frac{1}{4} + \frac{1}{4}$

Ⓑ $\frac{1}{4} + \frac{1}{4} + \frac{1}{4} + \frac{1}{4} + \frac{1}{4} + \frac{1}{4} + \frac{1}{4} + \frac{1}{4} + \frac{1}{4} + \frac{1}{4} + \frac{1}{4}$

Ⓒ $\frac{1}{4} + \frac{1}{4} + \frac{1}{4} + \frac{1}{4} + \frac{1}{4} + \frac{1}{4} + \frac{1}{4} + \frac{1}{4} + \frac{1}{4} + \frac{1}{4} + \frac{1}{4} + \frac{1}{4}$

Ⓓ $\frac{3}{4} + \frac{4}{4} + \frac{2}{4} + \frac{1}{4} + \frac{2}{4}$

Ⓔ $\frac{5}{4} + \frac{5}{4} + \frac{1}{4}$

Ⓕ $\frac{3}{4} + \frac{3}{4} + \frac{3}{4} + \frac{2}{4}$

DURING THE VIDEO: Pause after each "character" solves the problem and jot down quick notes to help you remember what they did correctly or incorrectly.

Character #1 _____	Character #2 _____
Character #3 _____	**Character #4** _____

193

TAKING ON THE B.E.S.T.

Math Misconception Mystery (PAGE 2)

AFTER THE VIDEO: Discuss and analyze their answers.

The most reasonable answer belongs to Character # _____ because

_____

_____

_____

_____

(Justify how this character's work makes sense.)

Let's help the others:

	Character #___:	Character #___:	Character #___:
What did this character do that was correct?			
Identify their error			
What do they need to know to understand for next time?			

TAKING ON THE B.E.S.T.

Find the sum and difference of each expression. Include a visual model to represent each equation.

1

$$\frac{4}{6} + \frac{2}{6}$$

$$\frac{4}{6} - \frac{2}{6}$$

2

$$\frac{11}{16} + \frac{4}{16}$$

$$\frac{11}{16} - \frac{4}{16}$$

3

$$\frac{7}{12} + \frac{4}{12}$$

$$\frac{7}{12} - \frac{4}{12}$$

195

© McCarthy Math Academy

MA.4.FR.2.2 | **Extra Practice #1** | **Basic Addition and Subtraction of Fractions**

Find the sum and difference of each expression. Include a visual model to represent each equation.

1

$$\frac{5}{10} + \frac{4}{10}$$

$$\frac{5}{10} - \frac{4}{10}$$

2

$$\frac{6}{8} + \frac{4}{8}$$

$$\frac{6}{8} - \frac{4}{8}$$

3

$$\frac{6}{12} + \frac{6}{12}$$

$$\frac{6}{12} - \frac{6}{12}$$

196

TAKING ON THE B.E.S.T.

MA.4.FR.2.2  **Video Lesson** | **Addition of Fractions with Like Denominators**

Find the sum of each expression. Include a visual model to represent each sum.

1 6 fifths + 3 fifths

2 13 eighths + 12 eighths

3 $1\frac{3}{4} + 2\frac{2}{4}$

TAKING ON THE B.E.S.T.

| Extra Practice #2 | **Addition of Fractions with Like Denominators**

Find the sum of each expression. Include a visual model to represent each sum.

1 7 thirds + 9 thirds

2 5 fourths + 5 fourths

3 $2\frac{1}{3} + 1\frac{2}{3}$

198

TAKING ON THE B.E.S.T.

Find the difference of each expression. Include a visual model to represent each difference.

1   8 thirds – 2 thirds

2   17 sixths – 3 sixths

3 $3\frac{1}{3} - 1\frac{2}{3}$

199

TAKING ON THE B.E.S.T.

Find the difference of each expression. Include a visual model to represent each difference.

1 12 fifths – 2 fifths

2 15 eighths – 4 eighths

3 $2\frac{2}{6} - \frac{4}{6}$

TAKING ON THE B.E.S.T.

MA.4.FR.2.2 | **Math Missions** | **Add and Subtract Fractions with Like Denominators**

PART ONE

Use the cards to create an expression to find the difference of two mixed numbers. Then find the value of your expression.

CARDS

1 2 3 4 5
6 7 8 9 10

PART TWO

Find the sum of the mixed numbers you created above. Use a visual model to represent how you can find the sum.

201

TAKING ON THE B.E.S.T.

Math Misconception Mystery
(PAGE 1)

BEFORE THE VIDEO: Solve the problem on your own.

Find the sum of the fractions below. Then, find the difference.

$$3\frac{3}{8} + \frac{7}{8}$$

$$3\frac{3}{8} - \frac{7}{8}$$

DURING THE VIDEO: Pause after each "character" solves the problem and jot down quick notes to help you remember what they did correctly or incorrectly.

Character #1 _____

Character #2 _____

Character #3 _____

Character #4 _____

TAKING ON THE B.E.S.T.

Math Misconception Mystery
(PAGE 2)

AFTER THE VIDEO: Discuss and analyze their answers.

The most reasonable answer belongs to Character # _____ because

_____

_____

_____

_____

(Justify how this character's work makes sense.)

Let's help the others:

	Character #___:	Character #___:	Character #___:
What did this character do that was correct?			
Identify their error			
What do they need to know to understand for next time?			

203

TAKING ON THE B.E.S.T.

| Video Lesson | **Add Fractions with Denominators of 10 and 100**

Create a visual model to find the sum of the two fractions.

1 $\dfrac{4}{10} + \dfrac{51}{100} = \boxed{}$

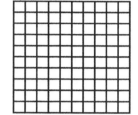 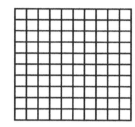

3 $\dfrac{38}{100} + \dfrac{2}{10} = \boxed{}$

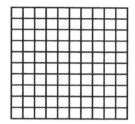 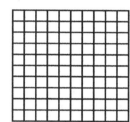

2 $\dfrac{5}{100} + \dfrac{5}{10} = \boxed{}$

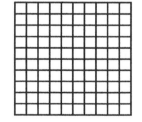 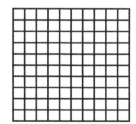

4 $\dfrac{9}{10} + \dfrac{23}{100} = \boxed{}$

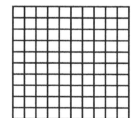 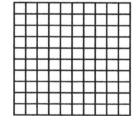

204

TAKING ON THE B.E.S.T.

MA.4.FR.2.3 | **Extra Practice #1** | **Add Fractions with Denominators of 10 and 100**

Create a visual model to find the sum of the two fractions.

1 $\dfrac{6}{10} + \dfrac{25}{100} =$ ☐

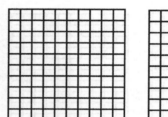 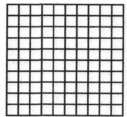

3 $\dfrac{42}{100} + \dfrac{3}{10} =$ ☐

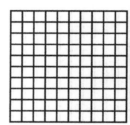 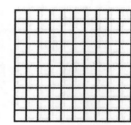

2 $\dfrac{14}{100} + \dfrac{7}{10} =$ ☐

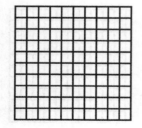 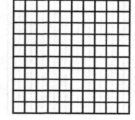

4 $\dfrac{8}{10} + \dfrac{37}{100} =$ ☐

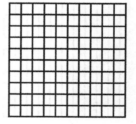 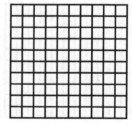

205

TAKING ON THE B.E.S.T.

MA.4.FR.2.3 | **Extra Practice #2** | **Add Fractions with Denominators of 10 and 100**

Create a visual model to find the sum of the two fractions.

1 $\dfrac{2}{10} + \dfrac{66}{100} = \boxed{}$

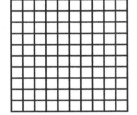 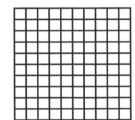

3 $\dfrac{54}{100} + \dfrac{1}{10} = \boxed{}$

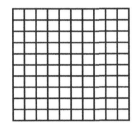 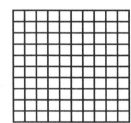

2 $\dfrac{3}{100} + \dfrac{3}{10} = \boxed{}$

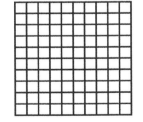 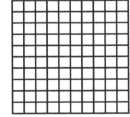

4 $\dfrac{7}{10} + \dfrac{46}{100} = \boxed{}$

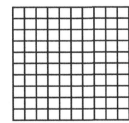 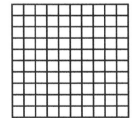

TAKING ON THE B.E.S.T.

MA.4.FR.2.3 | **Math Missions** | **Add and Subtract Fractions with Like Denominators**

PART ONE

Eduardo walks $\frac{7}{10}$ mile on Monday. Two days later, he walks $\frac{22}{100}$ mile. How far did Eduardo walk altogether? Use the 10x10 grids below to create a visual model. Then, explain your thinking in words on the lines below.

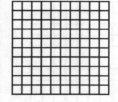 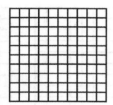

_____

_____

_____

_____

_____

_____

_____

_____

PART TWO

The following week, Eduardo walks $\frac{49}{100}$ mile on Tuesday and $\frac{8}{10}$ mile on Wednesday. Combine all four of his walks to determine the total distance that he walked over the period of two weeks. Explain your thinking on the lines below.

_____

_____

_____

_____

TAKING ON THE B.E.S.T.

**Math Misconception Mystery
(PAGE 1)**

BEFORE THE VIDEO: Solve the problem on your own.

Find the sum of the fractions below.

$$\frac{6}{10} + \frac{7}{100}$$

DURING THE VIDEO: Pause after each "character" solves the problem and jot down quick notes to help you remember what they did correctly or incorrectly.

Character #1 _____	Character #2 _____
Character #3 _____	**Character #4** _____

TAKING ON THE B.E.S.T.

MA.4.FR.2.3

Math Misconception Mystery
(PAGE 2)

AFTER THE VIDEO: Discuss and analyze their answers.

The most reasonable answer belongs to Character # _____ because

_____

_____

_____

_____

(Justify how this character's work makes sense.)

Let's help the others:

	Character #___:	Character #___:	Character #___:
What did this character do that was correct?			
Identify their error			
What do they need to know to understand for next time?			

209

TAKING ON THE B.E.S.T.

  Video Lesson | **Multiply a Whole Number by a Fraction**

Multiply each whole number by a fraction. Model with a visual area model, number line, and repeated addition.

1 $3 \times \dfrac{1}{2}$

NUMBER LINE

AREA MODEL	CONNECT TO REPEATED ADDITION

2 $4 \times \dfrac{2}{3}$

NUMBER LINE

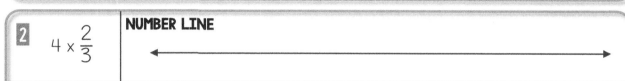

AREA MODEL	CONNECT TO REPEATED ADDITION

3 $5 \times \dfrac{3}{4}$

NUMBER LINE

AREA MODEL	CONNECT TO REPEATED ADDITION

TAKING ON THE B.E.S.T.

MA.4.FR.2.4 | **Extra Practice #1** | **Multiply a Whole Number by a Fraction**

Multiply each whole number by a fraction. Model with a visual area model, number line, and repeated addition.

1 $4 \times \frac{1}{2}$

NUMBER LINE

$\longleftrightarrow$

AREA MODEL

CONNECT TO REPEATED ADDITION

2 $5 \times \frac{2}{5}$

NUMBER LINE

$\longleftrightarrow$

AREA MODEL

CONNECT TO REPEATED ADDITION

3 $6 \times \frac{3}{6}$

NUMBER LINE

$\longleftrightarrow$

AREA MODEL

CONNECT TO REPEATED ADDITION

211

TAKING ON THE B.E.S.T.

  Video Lesson | **Multiply a Fraction by a Whole Number**

Multiply each fraction by a whole number. Model with a visual area model, number line, and repeated addition.

---

1 $\frac{1}{8} \times 4$

NUMBER LINE

AREA MODEL	CONNECT TO REPEATED ADDITION

---

2 $\frac{10}{12} \times 5$

NUMBER LINE

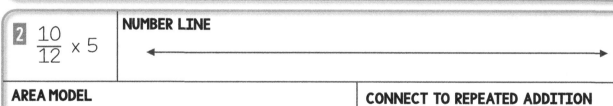

AREA MODEL	CONNECT TO REPEATED ADDITION

---

3 $\frac{5}{6} \times 3$

NUMBER LINE

AREA MODEL	CONNECT TO REPEATED ADDITION

TAKING ON THE B.E.S.T.

| Extra Practice #2 | **Multiply a Fraction by a Whole Number**

Multiply each fraction by a whole number. Model with a visual area model, number line, and repeated addition.

---

1 $\frac{4}{12} \times 3$

NUMBER LINE

$\longleftrightarrow$

AREA MODEL	CONNECT TO REPEATED ADDITION

---

2 $\frac{8}{12} \times 2$

NUMBER LINE

$\longleftrightarrow$

AREA MODEL	CONNECT TO REPEATED ADDITION

---

3 $\frac{7}{8} \times 4$

NUMBER LINE

$\longleftrightarrow$

AREA MODEL	CONNECT TO REPEATED ADDITION

213

TAKING ON THE B.E.S.T.

MA.4.FR.2.4  Video Lesson | **Multiply Mixed Numbers by a Whole Number**

Find the product of each expression .

1 $2\frac{3}{4} \times 4$

2 $3 \times 4\frac{1}{6}$

3 $8\frac{1}{2} \times 5$

TAKING ON THE B.E.S.T.

Extra Practice #3

Multiply Mixed Numbers by a Whole Number

Find the product of each expression.

1. $3\frac{2}{8} \times 5$

2. $2 \times 6\frac{1}{8}$

3. $5\frac{1}{2} \times 6$

215

TAKING ON THE B.E.S.T.

| MA.4.FR.2.4 | Math Missions | Multiply Fractions by Whole Numbers |

PART ONE

Tommy drinks $\frac{3}{4}$ gallon of water each day. How much water will he have consumed after 7 days (in gallons)? Create a visual area model and a number line representation this situation.

PART TWO

Martha drinks $\frac{2}{3}$ gallon of water each day. She says that she drinks $\frac{10}{15}$ gallon after 5 days. Explain Martha's error on the lines below.

_____

_____

_____

_____

_____

TAKING ON THE B.E.S.T.

Math Misconception Mystery
(PAGE 1)

BEFORE THE VIDEO: Solve the problem on your own.

> Find the product of the expression below.
>
> $3 \times \dfrac{7}{12}$

DURING THE VIDEO: Pause after each "character" solves the problem and jot down quick notes to help you remember what they did correctly or incorrectly.

Character #1 _____	Character #2 _____
Character #3 _____	**Character #4** _____

TAKING ON THE B.E.S.T.

Math Misconception Mystery (PAGE 2)

AFTER THE VIDEO: Discuss and analyze their answers.

The most reasonable answer belongs to Character # _____ because

_____

_____

_____

_____

(Justify how this character's work makes sense.)

Let's help the others:

	Character #___:	Character #___:	Character #___:
What did this character do that was correct?			
Identify their error			
What do they need to know to understand for next time?			

218

TAKING ON THE B.E.S.T.

1 Blake earns $17 a week babysitting. If he saves all of his money for 12 weeks, how much money will he have?

2 Rosita earns three times as much as Blake.

How much does Rosita earn each week?

If Rosita saves all of her money for 12 weeks, how much money will she have?

219

MA.4.AR.1.1 | **Extra Practice #1** | **Multiplication Word Problems**

---

1 Denny reads 26 pages a day. How many pages will he have read after 50 days?

---

2 Stephanie reads twice as much as Denny.

How many pages does she read a day?

How many pages will she have read after 50 days?

TAKING ON THE B.E.S.T.

1 Jermaine has 23 strawberries to make dessert for his family. Each dessert requires 4 strawberries. How many strawberries are leftover?

2 Mr. Sinkle has $33 in his wallet. He wants to give his 2 children an equal amount for completing their chores this week. How much money will each child receive?

221

TAKING ON THE B.E.S.T.

1 Ruby is creating Blessing Bags to help people who need it. She has 52 bottles of hand sanitizer. She wants each Blessing Bag to have 3 bottles of hand sanitizer. How many bottles will she have left over?

2 Brad bakes 10 pizzas for eight people to enjoy. If each person eats the same amount of pizza, how much pizza will each person consume?

222

TAKING ON THE B.E.S.T.

  **Video Lesson** | **Division Word Problems with Remainders - Round it, Drop it!**

1 The 4th graders at Happy Days Elementary are taking a field trip to the science museum. There are 47 students going on the field trip. Each vehicle can transport 4 students. How many vehicles are needed to transport all of the students?

2 Alanis has $80 to spend on cupcakes. Each cupcake costs $3. How many cupcakes can she purchase?

223

TAKING ON THE B.E.S.T.

1 The 4th graders at Happy Days Elementary are visited by a guest speaker. They must sit six students to a table. If there are 45 students, how many tables will be needed?

2 Hugo has 86 green tomatoes to make his famous tasty sandwich. If each sandwich needs 4 green tomatoes, how many sandwiches can he make?

TAKING ON THE B.E.S.T.

Math Missions

Word Problems with Multiplication and Division

PART ONE

Jermika orders 14 calculators for $21 each. How much does she spend?

PART TWO

Kuani spends spends four times as much as Jermika because he purchases 14 calculators with advanced capabilities. How much does Kuani spend on calculators?

PART THREE

Mrs. Depriest has $85 to purchase calculators for her students. Each calculator costs $10. Mrs. Depriest says that she can purchase $8\frac{5}{10}$ calculators. Explain her error on the lines below.

_____

_____

_____

_____

_____

TAKING ON THE B.E.S.T.

Math Misconception Mystery
(PAGE 1)

BEFORE THE VIDEO: Solve the problem on your own.

Dwayne has a $50 gift card to spend at a clothing store. How many $9 shirts can he buy?

DURING THE VIDEO: Pause after each "character" solves the problem and jot down quick notes to help you remember what they did correctly or incorrectly.

Character #1 _____

Character #2 _____

Character #3 _____

Character #4 _____

TAKING ON THE B.E.S.T.

Math Misconception Mystery
(PAGE 2)

AFTER THE VIDEO: Discuss and analyze their answers.

The most reasonable answer belongs to Character # _____ because

_____

_____

_____

_____

(Justify how this character's work makes sense.)

Let's help the others:			
	Character #___:	Character #___:	Character #___:
What did this character do that was correct?			
Identify their error			
What do they need to know to understand for next time?			

227

© McCarthy Math Academy

1 Barney loves carrot and pickle sandwiches. He makes three sandwiches to share with his buddy, Bob. Pretty soon, they are stuffed with $1\frac{1}{4}$ sandwiches remaining. What fraction of the carrot and pickle sandwiches did they eat?

2 Georgia studies for $1\frac{2}{4}$ hours on Monday, $2\frac{1}{4}$ hours on Tuesday, and $3\frac{3}{4}$ hours on Wednesday for her test on Thursday. How much time did she study altogether?

TAKING ON THE B.E.S.T.

1 Mr. Looky has two pieces of string. The first string is $4\frac{1}{8}$ inches. The second string is $1\frac{7}{8}$ inches longer. How much string does she have in all?

2 Hailey plans to drink $5\frac{3}{8}$ gallons of water this week. So far, she has consumed $3\frac{5}{8}$ gallons of water. How much water must she drink to reach her goal?

TAKING ON THE B.E.S.T.

1 Pedro orders nine pizzas for his birthday party. After the party, $2\frac{2}{10}$ pizza is left. How much pizza was consumed during the party?

2 Kesha practices singing for $2\frac{3}{6}$ hours the first week in March. The second week in March, she practices for $\frac{5}{6}$ of an hour. How much time did she practice so far in March?

230

TAKING ON THE B.E.S.T.

MA.4.AR.1.2 | **Math Missions** | **Add & Subtract Real-World Problems with Fractions and Mixed Numbers**

PART ONE

Waldo bought two bags of onions at the store. Each bag weighed $3\frac{3}{6}$ pounds. What is the total weight of onions that Waldo buys from the store?

PART TWO

Waldo uses $1\frac{4}{6}$ pounds of onions to make a huge batch of spaghetti sauce for his family reunion. He will still need more onions for a salad. How many pounds of onions will he have for his salad?

PART THREE

Create and solve a real-world problem for the equation: $2\frac{2}{5} + ? = 4\frac{1}{5}$

_____

_____

_____

_____

_____

TAKING ON THE B.E.S.T.

Math Misconception Mystery
(PAGE 1)

BEFORE THE VIDEO: Solve the problem on your own.

Reba reads $\frac{3}{12}$ of her book in the morning and $\frac{3}{12}$ of her book at night. What fraction of her book does she have left to read?

DURING THE VIDEO: Pause after each "character" solves the problem and jot down quick notes to help you remember what they did correctly or incorrectly.

Character #1 _____

Character #2 _____

Character #3 _____

Character #4 _____

TAKING ON THE B.E.S.T.

MA.4.AR.I.2 | Math Misconception Mystery (PAGE 2)

AFTER THE VIDEO: Discuss and analyze their answers.

The most reasonable answer belongs to Character # _____ because

_____

_____

_____

_____

(Justify how this character's work makes sense.)

Let's help the others:

	Character #___:	Character #___:	Character #___:
What did this character do that was correct?			
Identify their error			
What do they need to know to understand for next time?			

233

TAKING ON THE B.E.S.T.

  **Video Lesson** | **Multiply Whole Numbers by Fractions (Creating Word Problems)**

1 Create and solve a real-world problem based on the equation below. Include a visual.

$$3 \times \frac{1}{4} = n$$

_____

_____

_____

_____

_____

_____

2 Create and solve a real-world problem based on the equation below. Include a visual.

$$\frac{1}{4} \times 3 = n$$

_____

_____

_____

_____

_____

_____

234

TAKING ON THE B.E.S.T.

1 Create and solve a real-world problem based on the equation below. Include a visual.

$$4 \times \frac{2}{5} = n$$

_____

_____

_____

_____

_____

_____

2 Create and solve a real-world problem based on the equation below. Include a visual.

$$\frac{2}{5} \times 4 = n$$

_____

_____

_____

_____

_____

_____

TAKING ON THE B.E.S.T.

MA.4.AR.I.3  **Video Lesson** | **Multiply Whole Numbers by Fractions (Creating and Solving Equations)**

---

1 Michael is baking three batches of brownies. Each batch requires $\frac{3}{8}$ teaspoon of vanilla. How many teaspoons of vanilla does Michael need to make all three batches? Create an equation and solve. Include a visual representation.

---

2 Sarah has completed $\frac{6}{10}$ of her 4 mile run. How far has she traveled so far? Create an equation and solve. Include a visual representation.

236

1 The Smith Family is enjoying their first family cruise. So far, they have completed $\frac{2}{3}$ of their 6-day cruise. How many days have they been on the cruise? Create an equation and solve. Include a visual representation.

2 Stacy's mom packs snack bags for an afternoon at the park. She makes 4 snack bags, one for each of her children. In each bag, she packs $\frac{1}{10}$ pound of grapes. What is the total amount of grapes that she packs for the afternoon at the park? Create an equation and solve. Include a visual representation.

MA.4.AR.I.3	Math Missions	Word Problems: Multiply Whole Numbers by Fractions

PART ONE

Trina says $\frac{1}{2} \times 5$ can be represented as "5 days of running for one-half of an hour." Explain Trina's error.

_____

_____

_____

_____

PART TWO

Create a real-world scenario that correctly represents the equation $\frac{1}{2} \times 5 = n$.

_____

_____

_____

_____

PART THREE

Use a visual representation to model your correct scenario and solve.

238

TAKING ON THE B.E.S.T.

Math Misconception Mystery
(PAGE 1)

BEFORE THE VIDEO: Solve the problem on your own.

> Mr. Snooze needs lots of mushrooms for a recipe. At the grocery store, he picks up 7 packages of mushrooms. Each package weighs $\frac{2}{8}$ pound. What is the total weight of mushrooms that Mr. Snooze purchases from the store?

DURING THE VIDEO: Pause after each "character" solves the problem and jot down quick notes to help you remember what they did correctly or incorrectly.

Character #1 _____

Character #2 _____

Character #3 _____

Character #4 _____

239

TAKING ON THE B.E.S.T.

MA.4.AR.1.3 | **Math Misconception Mystery (PAGE 2)**

AFTER THE VIDEO: Discuss and analyze their answers.

The most reasonable answer belongs to Character # _____ because

_____

_____

_____

_____

(Justify how this character's work makes sense.)

Let's help the others:

	Character #___:	Character #___:	Character #___:
What did this character do that was correct?			
Identify their error			
What do they need to know to understand for next time?			

240

© McCarthy Math Academy

TAKING ON THE B.E.S.T.

Determine whether each equation is true or false. Explain your thinking on the lines provided.

1 $3 \times 8 = 144 \div 12$

_____
_____
_____
_____
_____
_____

2 $27 + 94 = 11 \times 12$

_____
_____
_____
_____
_____
_____

3 $96 \div 8 = 30 - 18$

_____
_____
_____
_____
_____
_____

241

MA.4.AR.2.1 | **Extra Practice #1** | **True and False Equations**

Determine whether each equation is true or false. Explain your thinking on the lines provided.

1 $100 - 68 = 8 \times 4$

_____
_____
_____
_____
_____
_____

2 $108 \div 9 = 4 + 4 + 4$

_____
_____
_____
_____
_____
_____
_____

3 $3 \times 3 \times 3 = 27 \div 3$

_____
_____
_____
_____
_____
_____

TAKING ON THE B.E.S.T.

Extra Practice #2 **True and False Equations**

Determine whether each equation is true or false. Explain your thinking on the lines provided.

1 $48 - 8 - 8 - 8 - 8 - 8 - 8 = 48 \div 8$

_____
_____
_____
_____
_____
_____

2 $8 \times 8 = 8 + 8 + 8 + 8 + 8 + 8 + 8 + 8$

_____
_____
_____
_____
_____
_____

3 $42 \div 6 = 42 \div 7$

_____
_____
_____
_____
_____
_____

TAKING ON THE B.E.S.T.

MA.4.AR.2.1 | **Math Missions** | **True and False Equations**

Use the cards for each task. You can use the cards more than once.

CARDS

3 4 6
8 9 12

PART ONE

Create an equation that is true. Explain how you know it is true.

[ ] x [ ] = [ ] x [ ]   _____
                          _____
                          _____
                          _____
                          _____
                          _____

PART ONE

Create an equation that is false. Explain how you know it is false.

[ ] + [ ] = [ ] - [ ]   _____
                          _____
                          _____
                          _____
                          _____
                          _____

TAKING ON THE B.E.S.T.

MA.4.AR.2.1

Math Misconception Mystery (PAGE 1)

BEFORE THE VIDEO: Solve the problem on your own.

> Determine whether the equation below is true or false.
>
> 200 - 128 = 3 x 4 x 6

DURING THE VIDEO: Pause after each "character" solves the problem and jot down quick notes to help you remember what they did correctly or incorrectly.

Character #1 _____	Character #2 _____
Character #3 _____	**Character #4** _____

TAKING ON THE B.E.S.T.

MA.4.AR.2.1 | **Math Misconception Mystery (PAGE 2)**

AFTER THE VIDEO: Discuss and analyze their answers.

The most reasonable answer belongs to Character # _____ because

_____

_____

_____

_____

(Justify how this character's work makes sense.)

Let's help the others:

	Character #___:	Character #___:	Character #___:
What did this character do that was correct?			
Identify their error			
What do they need to know to understand for next time?			

TAKING ON THE B.E.S.T.

1   Annalise is 3 years old. Her sister, Selena, is 6 times as old as Annalise. Write an equation to represent how old Selena, s, is. Then solve for the unknown value, s.

2   A local children's theater is hosting a family–friendly comedy show. Tickets for each show cost $8. The Melnyk family spends $48. How many tickets, t, did the Melnyk family purchase? Write an equation to represent this scenario. Then solve for the unknown value, t.

1 Vladymyr completes 64 multiplication problems in three minutes. This is 8 times as many problems that Niran, *n*, completes. Write an equation to represent this scenario. Then solve for the unknown value, *n*.

2 The De Leon family goes out for milkshakes. The six family members each order a chocolate milkshake. Determine the total cost, *c*, if each milkshake cost $4. Write an equation to represent this scenario. Then, solve for the unknown value, *c*.

248

TAKING ON THE B.E.S.T.

1 Nevaeh purchases a bag of oranges from the grocery store for $15. This is triple the cost she spends for a bag, *b*, of oranges from the local farm stand. Write an equation to determine the cost of one bag of oranges, *b*, from the local farm stand. Then, solve for the unknown value.

2 Gabriella runs 5 miles a week. Her cousin, Jorge, runs 50 miles a week. Write an equation to determine how many more times, *t*, Jorge runs each week than Gabriella. Then, solve for the unknown value.

MA.4.AR.2.2 | **Math Missions** | **Create Equations to Determine the Unknown Value**

Henry reads 6 pages each day. Liam reads double the amount of pages that Henry reads. Trent reads triple the amount that Liam reads.

PART ONE

Create an equation to determine the number of pages Liam, L, reads. Then, solve for the unknown value. Include a visual representation to model the scenario.

PART TWO

Create an equation to determine the number of pages Trent, T, reads. Then, solve for the unknown value. Include a visual representation to model the scenario.

MA.4.AR.2.2	Math Misconception Mystery (PAGE 1)

BEFORE THE VIDEO: Solve the problem on your own.

Janet buys four pairs of jeans for $48. Which equations below represents how much Janet spends for each pair of jeans, *j*?

Ⓐ $j = 48 \times 4$

Ⓑ $48 = j \times 4$

Ⓒ $48 = j + 4$

Ⓓ $j = 48 \div 4$

Ⓔ $48 = j \div 4$

DURING THE VIDEO: Pause after each "character" solves the problem and jot down quick notes to help you remember what they did correctly or incorrectly.

Character #1 _____

Character #2 _____

Character #3 _____

Character #4 _____

251

TAKING ON THE B.E.S.T.

MA.4.AR.2.2	Math Misconception Mystery (PAGE 2)

AFTER THE VIDEO: Discuss and analyze their answers.

The most reasonable answer belongs to Character # _____ because

_____

_____

_____

_____

(Justify how this character's work makes sense.)

Let's help the others:

	Character #___:	Character #___:	Character #___:
What did this character do that was correct?			
Identify their error			
What do they need to know to understand for next time?			

252

TAKING ON THE B.E.S.T.

  Video Lesson | **Prime, Composite, or Neither**

---

1 **PRIME NUMBERS:** Must have _____ factors.

COMPOSITE NUMBERS: Must have _____ factors.

0 AND 1 are _____

---

2 Find all the factor pairs for 12 to determine if it is prime or composite. Include arrays to represent the factor pair(s).

---

3 Find all the factor pairs for 13 to determine if it is prime or composite. Include arrays to represent the factor pair(s).

TAKING ON THE B.E.S.T.

1 **PRIME NUMBERS:** Must have _____ factors.

COMPOSITE NUMBERS: Must have _____ factors.

0 AND 1 are _____.

2 Find all the factor pairs for 9 to determine if it is prime or composite. Include arrays to represent the factor pair(s).

3 Find all the factor pairs for 17 to determine if it is prime or composite. Include arrays to represent the factor pair(s).

254

TAKING ON THE B.E.S.T.

MA.4.AR.3.1

Video Lesson

Find All Factors

Find all the factor pairs of each number. Determine if it is prime or composite.

1 15

2 43

3 55

TAKING ON THE B.E.S.T.

Find all the factor pairs of each number. Determine if it is prime or composite.

1 18

2 100

3 121

TAKING ON THE B.E.S.T.

  Video Lesson **Using Divisibility Rules**

FACTOR	DIVISIBILITY RULE
1	All numbers are divisible by 1.
2	Is it even?
3	Is the sum of the digits divisible by 3?
4	Is the 2-digit number in the tens and ones place divisible by 4?
5	Is the ones place 0 or 5?
6	Is it even? Is the sum of the digits divisible by 3?
9	Is the sum of the digits divisible by 9?

Find all the factor pairs of each number using the divisibility rules. Determine if it is prime or composite.

1 24

2 132

FACTOR	DIVISIBILITY RULE
1	All numbers are divisible by 1.
2	Is it even?
3	Is the sum of the digits divisible by 3?
4	Is the 2-digit number in the tens and ones place divisible by 4?
5	Is the ones place 0 or 5?
6	Is it even? Is the sum of the digits divisible by 3?
9	Is the sum of the digits divisible by 9?

Find all the factor pairs of each number using the divisibility rules. Determine if it is prime or composite.

1 51

2 144

TAKING ON THE B.E.S.T.

MA.4.AR.3.1	Math Missions	Factoring, Prime, and Composite Numbers

PART ONE

What are all the factors of 24? Include an array for each factor pair.

PART TWO

What are all the factors of 32? Include an array for each factor pair.

PART THREE

Amber says that 24, 32, 48 only the share the common factors 4 and 8. Do you agree with Amber? Explain your thinking.

_____

_____

_____

_____

259

TAKING ON THE B.E.S.T.

MA.4.AR.3.1 | Math Misconception Mystery (PAGE 1)

BEFORE THE VIDEO: Solve the problem on your own.

> Select all statements that are true about the number 36.
> Ⓐ All the factors of 36 are 1,2,3,6,12,18, and 36.
> Ⓑ All the factors of 36 are 1,2,3,4,6,9,12,18, and 36.
> Ⓒ 36 is a prime number.
> Ⓓ 36 is a composite number.
> Ⓔ 36 is neither prime nor composite.

DURING THE VIDEO: Pause after each "character" solves the problem and jot down quick notes to help you remember what they did correctly or incorrectly.

Character #1 _____	Character #2 _____
Character #3 _____	**Character #4** _____

260

TAKING ON THE B.E.S.T.

Math Misconception Mystery (PAGE 2)

AFTER THE VIDEO: Discuss and analyze their answers.

The most reasonable answer belongs to Character # _____ because _____

_____

_____

_____

(Justify how this character's work makes sense.)

Let's help the others:

	Character #___:	Character #___:	Character #___:
What did this character do that was correct?			
Identify their error			
What do they need to know to understand for next time?			

261

1 The first term in a pattern is 2. The pattern follows the rule "add 11." What are the next 5 terms in the pattern?

2 The first term in a pattern is 1. The pattern follows the rule "multiply by 6." What are the next 4 terms in the pattern?

3 The first term in a pattern is 400. The pattern follows the rule "subtract 98." What are the next 3 terms in the pattern?

TAKING ON THE B.E.S.T.

1 The first term in a pattern is 1. The pattern follows the rule "add 7." What are the next 5 terms in the pattern?

2 The first term in a pattern is 2. The pattern follows the rule "multiply by 5." What are the next 4 terms in the pattern?

3 The first term in a pattern is 240. The pattern follows the rule "divide by 2." What are the next 3 terms in the pattern?

TAKING ON THE B.E.S.T.

MA.4.AR.3.2 |  **Video Lesson** | **Determine Rules of Patterns and Extend**

1 A pattern is shown below.

20, 26, 32, 38,...

What is the rule of the pattern?

What are the next 3 terms?

2 A pattern is shown below.

99, 87, 75, 63, ...

What is the rule of the pattern?

Will the 7ᵗʰ term be odd or even?

3 A pattern is shown below.

_____, 256, 64, 16, 4, 1

What is the rule of the pattern?

What is the first term of the pattern?

264

© McCarthy Math Academy

TAKING ON THE B.E.S.T.

MA.4.AR.3.2 | Extra Practice #2 | Determine Rules of Patterns and Extend

1 A pattern is shown below.

2, 6, 18, 54,...

What is the rule of the pattern?

What are the next 2 terms?

2 A pattern is shown below.

2,500; 500; 100; 20; ...

What is the rule of the pattern?

Will the 5th term be odd or even?

3 A pattern is shown below.

40, 47, 54, 61, ...

What is the rule of the pattern?

What are the next 4 terms of the pattern?

1 A pattern is shown below.

What is the rule?

Will the 7th term be odd or even? Explain how you know.

2 A pattern is shown below.

What is the rule?

What will the fifth term look like? .

| MA.4.AR.3.2 | Extra Practice #3 | Patterns Challenge |

1 A pattern is shown below.

What is the rule?

Will the 6th term be odd or even? Explain how you know.

2 A pattern is shown below.

  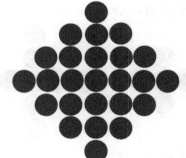

What is the rule?

How many circles will be in the 7th term? .

267

TAKING ON THE B.E.S.T.

Math Missions **Patterns**

PART ONE

A pattern is shown below.

___ , ___ , 70, 104, ___, 172, ____

What is the rule of the pattern?

Fill in the missing numbers.

Extend the pattern to include 3 more terms.

PART TWO

Create a pattern with the rule multiply by 3. Include 6 terms in your pattern. Are you terms odd, even, or both?

TAKING ON THE B.E.S.T.

Math Misconception Mystery
(PAGE I)

BEFORE THE VIDEO: Solve the problem on your own.

The first term in a pattern is 8. The pattern follows the rule, "add 5." Select all of the numbers below that are a term in the pattern.

Ⓐ 1
Ⓑ 4
Ⓒ 5
Ⓓ 13
Ⓔ 15
Ⓕ 28

DURING THE VIDEO: Pause after each "character" solves the problem and jot down quick notes to help you remember what they did correctly or incorrectly.

Character #1 _____

Character #2 _____

Character #3 _____

Character #4 _____

TAKING ON THE B.E.S.T.

Math Misconception Mystery
(PAGE 2)

AFTER THE VIDEO: Discuss and analyze their answers.

The most reasonable answer belongs to Character # _____ because

_____

_____

_____

_____

(Justify how this character's work makes sense.)

Let's help the others:

	Character #___:	Character #___:	Character #___:
What did this character do that was correct?			
Identify their error			
What do they need to know to understand for next time?			

TAKING ON THE B.E.S.T.

MA.4.M.1.1 |  Video Lesson | **Measuring Length**

---

1 List tools that are appropriate for measuring the length of an object.

---

2 What is the length of each object to the nearest millimeter?

C

B

A

0 cm 1 2 3 4 5 6 7 8 9 10 11 12

A: _____   B: _____   C: _____
   _____   _____   _____

This ruler is not drawn to scale.

---

3 What is the length of each object to the nearest $\frac{1}{8}$ and $\frac{1}{16}$ of an inch?

C

B

A

0 in 1 2 3 4 5 6

This ruler is not drawn to scale.

A: _____   B: _____   C: _____
   _____   _____   _____

271

TAKING ON THE B.E.S.T.

1   What is the length of each object to the nearest millimeter?

C

B

A

```
0 cm   1    2    3    4    5    6    7    8    9    10   11   12
```

A: _____   B: _____   C: _____

_____   _____   _____

This ruler is not drawn to scale.

2   What is the length of each object to the nearest $\frac{1}{8}$ and $\frac{1}{16}$ of an inch?

C

B

A

```
0 in    1      2      3      4      5      6
```

A: _____   B: _____   C: _____

_____   _____   _____

This ruler is not drawn to scale.

TAKING ON THE B.E.S.T.

MA.4.M.1.1 |  Video Lesson | **Measuring Liquid Volume**

1 List tools that are appropriate for measuring liquid volume.

2 Container A and B are both the same size, but are filled with different amounts. What is the volume of water in each container, in millimeters?

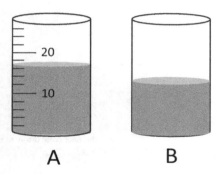

A

B

A: _____

B: _____

3 What is the liquid volume in the measuring cup to the nearest $\frac{1}{8}$ of a cup?

— 4 cups

— 3 cups

— 2 cups

— 1 cup

TAKING ON THE B.E.S.T.

1 Container A and B are both the same size, but are filled with different amounts. What is the volume of water in each container, in millimeters?

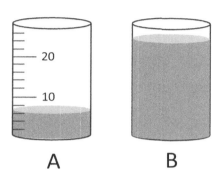

A   B

A: _____

B: _____

2 What is the liquid volume in each measuring cup to the nearest $\frac{1}{8}$ of a cup?

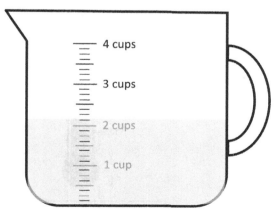

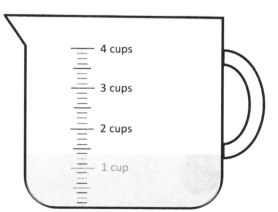

274

© McCarthy Math Academy

TAKING ON THE B.E.S.T.

MA.4.M.1.1 | Video Lesson | **Measuring Temperature**

1 List tools that are appropriate for measuring temperature.

2 Find the measure of each thermometer to the nearest degree.

A

B

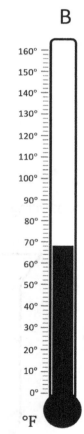

C

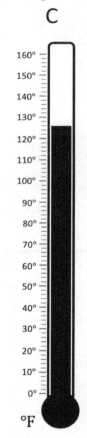

TAKING ON THE B.E.S.T.

Find the measure of each thermometer to the nearest degree.

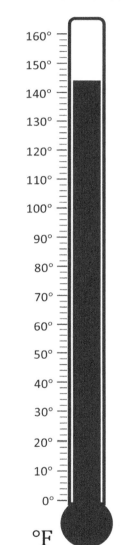

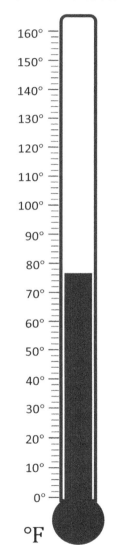

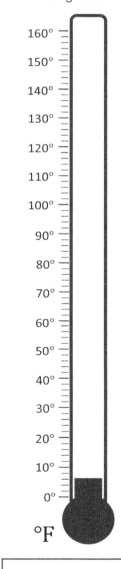

°F   °F   °F

TAKING ON THE B.E.S.T.

1 What is the difference between weight and mass?

_____

_____

2 Find the weight of the object according to the scale, in pounds.

3 What can you determine from the balance?

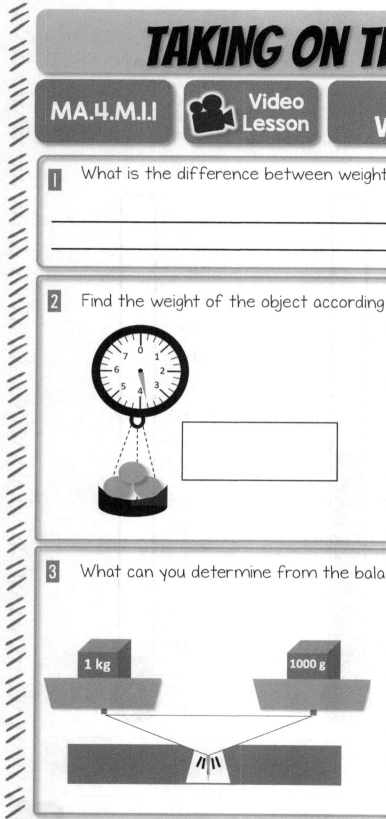

_____

_____

_____

_____

_____

_____

277

TAKING ON THE B.E.S.T.

MA.4.M.1.1 | **Extra Practice #4** | **Measuring Weight and Mass**

1 Jamie says that his apple has a mass of 85 grams, which would have a different mass if it was on the moon. Do you agree or disagree?

_____

_____

2 Find the weight of the object according to the scale, in pounds.

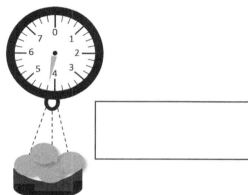

3 What can you determine from the balance?

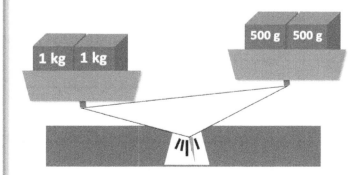

_____

_____

_____

_____

_____

278

TAKING ON THE B.E.S.T.

MA.4.M.1.1	Math Missions	Measure Length, Liquid Volume, and Temperature

PART ONE

Annette poured $3\frac{5}{8}$ cups of warm water into a measuring cup. Then, she poured 14 milliliters into a graduated cylinder. Draw a model of the exact water measurements in the measuring cup and graduated cylinder.

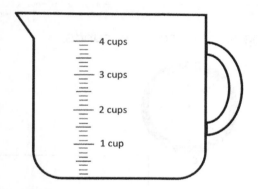 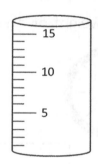

PART TWO

Next, Annette measured the temperature of the warm water. She says that the temperature is 112° F. Explain Annette's error. What is the correct temperature?

TAKING ON THE B.E.S.T.

Math Misconception Mystery (PAGE 1)

BEFORE THE VIDEO: Solve the problem on your own.

What is the length of the arrow to the nearest $\frac{1}{16}$ and $\frac{1}{8}$ of an inch?

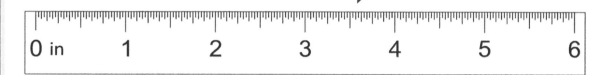

DURING THE VIDEO: Pause after each "character" solves the problem and jot down quick notes to help you remember what they did correctly or incorrectly.

Character #1 _____

Character #2 _____

Character #3 _____

Character #4 _____

280

TAKING ON THE B.E.S.T.

Math Misconception Mystery
(PAGE 2)

AFTER THE VIDEO: Discuss and analyze their answers.

The most reasonable answer belongs to Character # _____ because

_____

_____

_____

_____

(Justify how this character's work makes sense.)

Let's help the others:

	Character #___:	Character #___:	Character #___:
What did this character do that was correct?			
Identify their error			
What do they need to know to understand for next time?			

281

TAKING ON THE B.E.S.T.

1 Eugene has 24 feet of string. How many yards of string does Eugene have?

1 foot = 12 inches
1 yard = 3 feet

2 Alexa walks 4 kilometers. How many meters does Alexa walk?

1 meter = 100 centimeters
1 meter = 1000 millimeters
1 kilometer = 1000 meters

282

TAKING ON THE B.E.S.T.

MA.4.M.I.2	Extra Practice #1	Measurement Conversions: Length

1 How many inches are in 15 feet? How many yards are in 15 feet?

1 foot = 12 inches
1 yard = 3 feet

2 How many centimeters are in 5 meters?

1 meter = 100 centimeters
1 meter = 1000 millimeters
1 kilometer = 1000 meters

TAKING ON THE B.E.S.T.

1   Katie has 12 quarts of orange juice. How many gallons of orange juice does Katie have? How many cups of orange juice does Katie have?

> 1 pint = 2 cups
> 1 quart = 2 pints
> 1 gallon = 4 quarts

2   Daqwan needs $2\frac{1}{2}$ liters of water. How many milliliters of water does Daqwan have?

> 1 liter = 1000 milliliters

284

TAKING ON THE B.E.S.T.

1 Bethany has 22 pints of oil. How many cups of oil is this?

1 pint = 2 cups
1 quart = 2 pints
1 gallon = 4 quarts

2 Ricardo's mom asks him to pick up 8 liters of juice from the store. How many milliliters of juice should Ricardo pick up?

1 liter = 1000 milliliters

285

TAKING ON THE B.E.S.T.

  **Video Lesson** | **Measurement Conversions: Weight and Mass**

1 The Jackson's cart has a weight of 500 pounds. What is the weight in ounces?

1 pound = 16 ounces

2 Marty's dog has a mass of $4\frac{1}{2}$ kilograms. How many grams is this?

1 gram = 1000 milligrams
1 kilograms = 1000 grams

286

© McCarthy Math Academy

TAKING ON THE B.E.S.T.

1 A sloth weighs 144 ounces. How much does a sloth weigh in pounds?

1 pound = 16 ounces

2 A cat has a mass of $3\frac{1}{2}$ kilograms. What is the mass of the cat in grams?

1 gram = 1000 milligrams
1 kilograms = 1000 grams

287

© McCarthy Math Academy

TAKING ON THE B.E.S.T.

1 Dawson reads for 180 minutes. How long does Dawson read in hours?

1 minute = 60 seconds
1 hour = 60 minutes

2 How many seconds are in $4\frac{1}{2}$ minutes? How many seconds are in 2 hours?

1 minute = 60 seconds
1 hour = 60 minutes

288

TAKING ON THE B.E.S.T.

1 Marie runs a marathon in 5 hours. How many minutes did Marie run? How many seconds did Marie run?

> 1 minute = 60 seconds
> 1 hour = 60 minutes

2 How many hours are in 330 minutes? How many seconds are in 330 minutes?

> 1 minute = 60 seconds
> 1 hour = 60 minutes

289

TAKING ON THE B.E.S.T.

| MA.4.M.I.2 | Math Missions | Measurement Conversions |

This activity will require the following tools: a yard stick, a ruler, and measuring tape.

PART ONE

Use the tools to measure one length of your room. Place your recordings in the table below.

	Length of Room
Yards (to the nearest half of a yard)	
Ruler (to the nearest foot)	
Ruler (to the nearest centimeter)	
Measuring tape (in feet, inches)	

PART TWO

Which tool do you believe provided the most accurate measurement? Which tool provided the least accurate measurement? Record your thoughts on the lines below. Be sure to explain your thinking.

_____

_____

_____

_____

_____

TAKING ON THE B.E.S.T.

| MA.4.M.1.2 | Math Misconception Mystery (PAGE 1) |

BEFORE THE VIDEO: Solve the problem on your own.

Three lengths are provided below. Place them in order from longest to shortest.

| 2 yards | $7\frac{1}{4}$ feet | 70 inches |

1 foot = 12 inches
1 yard = 3 feet

DURING THE VIDEO: Pause after each "character" solves the problem and jot down quick notes to help you remember what they did correctly or incorrectly.

Character #1 _____

Character #2 _____

Character #3 _____

Character #4 _____

TAKING ON THE B.E.S.T.

MA.4.M.1.2	Math Misconception Mystery (PAGE 2)

AFTER THE VIDEO: Discuss and analyze their answers.

The most reasonable answer belongs to Character # _____ because

_____

_____

_____

_____

(Justify how this character's work makes sense.)

Let's help the others:

	Character #___:	Character #___:	Character #___:
What did this character do that was correct?			
Identify their error			
What do they need to know to understand for next time?			

TAKING ON THE B.E.S.T.

1 Terrell has soccer practice twice a week from a quarter til 4 until a half past 4. Kyle has soccer practice for three times longer than Terrell. How many minutes does Kyle have soccer practice each week?

2 It takes Connor $\frac{1}{3}$ hour to walk to school. If he walks round trip every day, how many minutes does he spend walking to school over the period of five days?

TAKING ON THE B.E.S.T.

MA.4.M.2.1 | **Extra Practice #1** | **Measurement Real-World Problems Involving Time**

1 Ms. Ruiz tutors for 45 minutes a day for 4 days of the week. How many hours does Ms. Ruiz tutor in a week?

2 Tony studies his multiplication facts for half an hour each day. His cousin studies her multiplication facts for a quarter hour each day. After three days, how many more minutes does Tony study compared to his cousin?

294

TAKING ON THE B.E.S.T.

1. On Monday, Nancy sprints 100 feet. Every day, she doubles the length she sprinted the day before. If she continues this pattern, how many feet will Nancy sprint on Friday?

2. Guiliana throws a baseball $10\frac{8}{10}$ meters. Paulo throws the same baseball $\frac{2}{10}$ meter farther than Guiliana. How far did Paulo throw the ball in centimeters?

TAKING ON THE B.E.S.T.

| Extra Practice #2 | Measurement Real-World Problems Involving Distance

1 Tracey's garden is shown below. What is the perimeter of her garden?

$3\frac{1}{4}$ yards

$2\frac{3}{4}$ yards

2 Last week, Mr. Santiago traveled 55 miles each day for three days. This week, he travels 469 miles more than he did last week. How many miles did he travel this week?

TAKING ON THE B.E.S.T.

The Singh family is going on a family vacation to a cabin in Tennessee from Fernandina Beach, Florida.

PART ONE

They left at 6:15 a.m. Their navigation system says that it will take 8 hours, 30 minutes to arrive at their cabin. If they plan to stop three times for 20 minute breaks, what time should they plan to arrive at their cabin?

PART TWO

The Signh family travels 817 miles to get to the cabin, and the same distance back. They also went exploring during their trip. If their odometer displays that they have traveled 1,948 miles, for how many miles were they exploring?

TAKING ON THE B.E.S.T.

Math Misconception Mystery
(PAGE 1)

BEFORE THE VIDEO: Solve the problem on your own.

David finishes cleaning his house at a quarter past 12 in the afternoon. It took him 36 minutes to clean his room, 12 minutes to fold and put away his laundry, and 39 minutes to clean the bathroom. If he took a 5 minute break to talk to his mom on the phone, what time did he begin cleaning?

DURING THE VIDEO: Pause after each "character" solves the problem and jot down quick notes to help you remember what they did correctly or incorrectly.

Character #1 _____

Character #2 _____

Character #3 _____

Character #4 _____

298

TAKING ON THE B.E.S.T.

Math Misconception Mystery
(PAGE 2)

AFTER THE VIDEO: Discuss and analyze their answers.

The most reasonable answer belongs to Character # _____ because

_____

_____

_____

_____

(Justify how this character's work makes sense.)

Let's help the others:

	Character #___:	Character #___:	Character #___:
What did this character do that was correct?			
Identify their error			
What do they need to know to understand for next time?			

299

TAKING ON THE B.E.S.T.

  **Video Lesson** **Real-World Problems with Money**

1 Drake has 2 ten-dollar bills, 3 five-dollar bills, 4 one-dollar bills, 3 quarters, 5 dimes, 2 nickels, and 9 pennies. He wants to purchase a shirt and pair of jeans for $40.00. Does he have enough?

2 For Matt's birthday, he received a twenty-dollar bill and a $25 gift card to his favorite restaurant. He goes out to dinner at his favorite restaurant, and the total cost of his dinner is 24.99. He includes a tip of $5.15. How much money will Matt have left after paying for his dinner?

3 Mrs. Wertz buys a key lime pie for $9.58 and a lemonade for $2.76. If she hands the cashier a ten dollar bill and a five dollar bill, what bills and coins could she receive back as change?

TAKING ON THE B.E.S.T.

| Real-World Problems with Money

1 Marta has 4 ten–dollar bills, 5 five–dollar bills, 8 one–dollar bills, 8 quarters, 7 dimes, 12 nickels, and 39 pennies. She wants to purchase 5 books for a total of $80.00. Does she have enough? Explain your reasoning.

2 For Mr. Keys birthday, he received 2 twenty–dollar bills and a $50 gift card to a clothing store. Mr. Keys chooses a few items from the clothing store for a total of $68.66. How much money will Mr. Keys have after he pays?

3 Carter buys a pack of paper towels for $8.36 and milk for $4.99. If he hands the cashier a twenty–dollar bill, what bills and coins could he receive back as change?

TAKING ON THE B.E.S.T.

1 Robyn has 3 twenty–dollar bills, 5 ten–dollar bills, 3 quarters, 4 dimes, 2 nickels, and 63 pennies. She receives some more money for running a few errands for her neighbors, and now she has exactly $200. How much money did she receive from her neighbors?

2 Luke purchases an item for $8.86. He does not want to receive any pennies in change. How much money could he give the cashier to make sure he doesn't receive pennies as change?

3 Andrea purchases two body boards for $12.99 each and a package of beach toys $5.77. She hands the cashier 2 twenty–dollar bills. What possible bills and coins could she receive back?

302

TAKING ON THE B.E.S.T.

MA.4.M.2.2 | **Math Missions** | **Measurement Real-World Problems**

Chelsea wants to purchase equipment to record videos. Below is the her list of equipment and the cost.

- ☐ Microphone = $13.98
- ☐ Camera = $496.87
- ☐ Lighting = $159.97
- ☐ Editing software = $45.99
- ☐ Tripod = $24.88

PART ONE

Chelsea has $315.45 in her savings account. Which equipment can she purchase now? Explain your thinking.

_____

_____

_____

_____

_____

PART TWO

How much money does Chelsea need to earn to purchase all of the equipment she wants?

_____

_____

_____

_____

_____

TAKING ON THE B.E.S.T.

Math Misconception Mystery
(PAGE 1)

BEFORE THE VIDEO: Solve the problem on your own.

> A slice of pizza costs $1.75 for one slice. Christian orders two slices of pizza and hands the cashier a five dollar bill. What bills and coins could he receive as change?

DURING THE VIDEO: Pause after each "character" solves the problem and jot down quick notes to help you remember what they did correctly or incorrectly.

Character #1 _____	Character #2 _____
Character #3 _____	**Character #4** _____

304

TAKING ON THE B.E.S.T.

Math Misconception Mystery
(PAGE 2)

AFTER THE VIDEO: Discuss and analyze their answers.

The most reasonable answer belongs to Character # _____ because

_____

_____

_____

_____

(Justify how this character's work makes sense.)

Let's help the others:

	Character #___:	Character #___:	Character #___:
What did this character do that was correct?			
Identify their error			
What do they need to know to understand for next time?			

305

Identify the correct name for each angle. Provide a brief description of each.

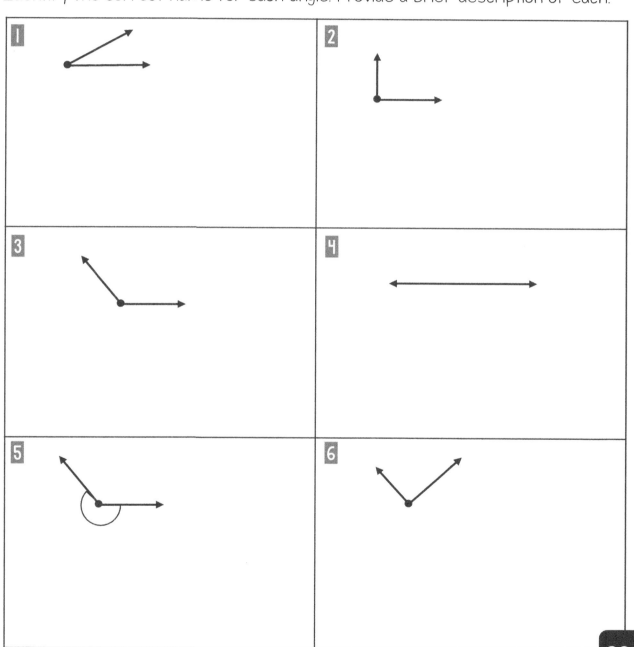

TAKING ON THE B.E.S.T.

Extra Practice #1

Geometry Vocabulary Introduction

Draw an example of each description.

1 obtuse angle	**2** straight angle
3 acute angle	**4** reflex angle
5 right angle	**6** a quadrilateral with 4 right angles

Determine the types and amount of angles in each two-dimensional figure.

1

❑ Acute angle(s)

❑ Right angle(s)

❑ Obtuse angle(s)

2

❑ Acute angle(s)

❑ Right angle(s)

❑ Obtuse angle(s)

3

❑ Acute angle(s)

❑ Right angle(s)

❑ Obtuse angle(s)

4

❑ Acute angle(s)

❑ Right angle(s)

❑ Obtuse angle(s)

TAKING ON THE B.E.S.T.

MA.4.GR.1.1 | **Extra Practice #2** | **Identifying Angles in Two-Dimensional Figures**

Determine whether each shape has the listed geometric features.

1

☐ Acute angle(s)

☐ Right angle(s)

☐ Obtuse angle(s)

2

☐ Acute angle(s)

☐ Right angle(s)

☐ Obtuse angle(s)

3

☐ Acute angle(s)

☐ Right angle(s)

☐ Obtuse angle(s)

4

☐ Acute angle(s)

☐ Right angle(s)

☐ Obtuse angle(s)

309

TAKING ON THE B.E.S.T.

PART ONE

Draw and label a triangle that has two acute angles and one obtuse angle.

PART TWO

Draw and label a triangle that has two acute angles and one right angle.

PART THREE

Draw and label a triangle that has three acute angles.

310

BEFORE THE VIDEO: Solve the problem on your own.

Which statement correctly describes the figure?

Ⓐ It has 5 acute angles

Ⓑ It has 5 obtuse angles

Ⓒ It is 5 right angles

Ⓓ It has an example of an acute, an obtuse, and a right angle.

DURING THE VIDEO: Pause after each "character" solves the problem and jot down quick notes to help you remember what they did correctly or incorrectly.

Character #1 _____	Character #2 _____
Character #3 _____	**Character #4** _____

311

MA.4.GR.I.I | **Math Misconception Mystery (PAGE 2)**

AFTER THE VIDEO: Discuss and analyze their answers.

The most reasonable answer belongs to Character # _____ because

_____

_____

_____

_____

(Justify how this character's work makes sense.)

Let's help the others:

	Character #___:	Character #___:	Character #___:
What did this character do that was correct?			
Identify their error			
What do they need to know to understand for next time?			

TAKING ON THE B.E.S.T.

Use the benchmark angles of 30°, 45°, 60°, 90°, and 180° to estimate each angle measure. Then, use a protractor to find the exact measure.

1

Estimate Angle
Measure: _____

Exact Angle
Measure: _____

2

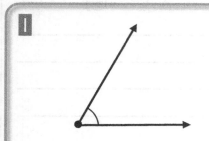

Estimate Angle
Measure: _____

Exact Angle
Measure: _____

3

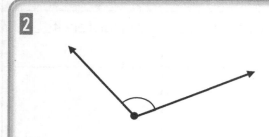

Estimate Angle
Measure: _____

Exact Angle
Measure: _____

TAKING ON THE B.E.S.T.

Use the benchmark angles of 30°, 45°, 60°, 90°, and 180° to estimate each angle measure. Then, use a protractor to find the exact measure.

1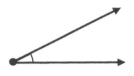

Estimate Angle
Measure: _____

Exact Angle
Measure: _____

2

Estimate Angle
Measure: _____

Exact Angle
Measure: _____

3

Estimate Angle
Measure: _____

Exact Angle
Measure: _____

TAKING ON THE B.E.S.T.

Use the standard and circle protractors to determine the exact measure of each angle.

1
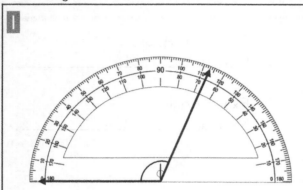

2
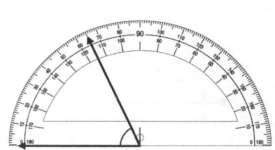

3
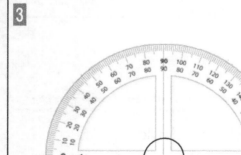

4
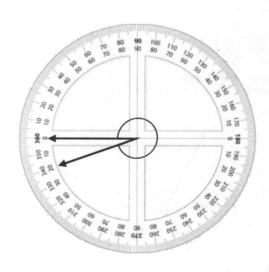

315

TAKING ON THE B.E.S.T.

MA.4.GR.1.2 | **Extra Practice #2** | **Estimate and Find Precise Angle Measurements**

Use the standard and circle protractors to determine the exact measure of each angle.

1 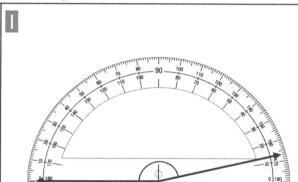	**2** 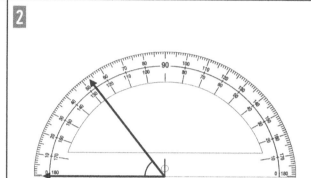
3 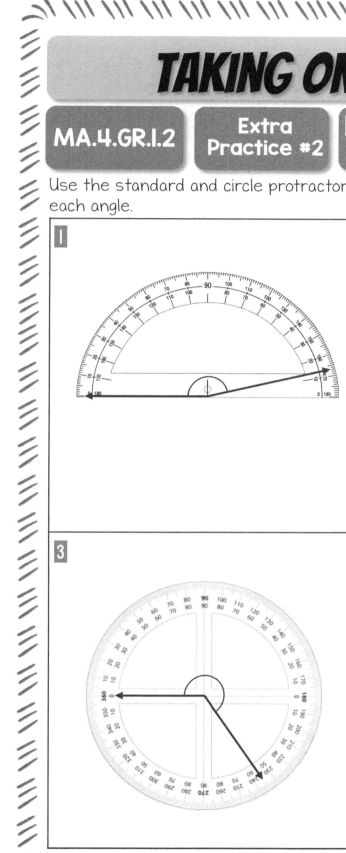	**4** 

TAKING ON THE B.E.S.T.

Video Lesson | **Draw Angles of Specified Measure**

Use the standard and circle protractors to draw the angles provided.

1 23° 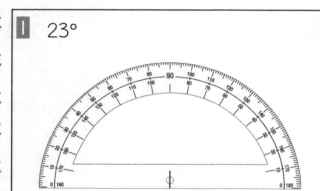	**2** 137° 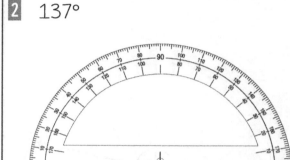
3 215° 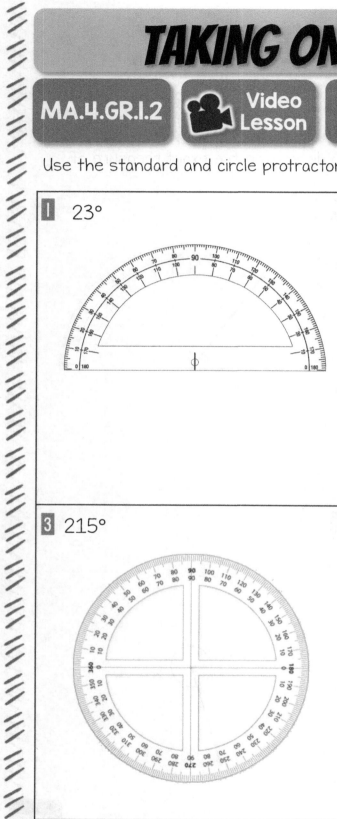	**4** 351° 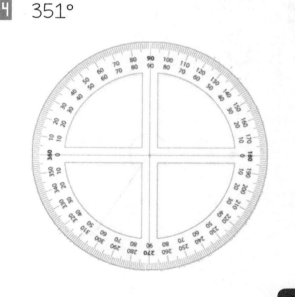

TAKING ON THE B.E.S.T.

Use the standard and circle protractors to draw the angles provided.

1 89°

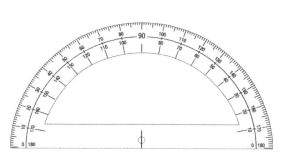

2 110°

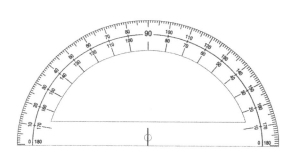

3 232°

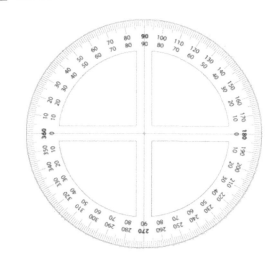

4 184°

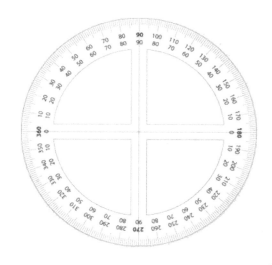

318

1 Find the exact measure of each angle. Which angles, when added together, make a right angle? Circle them.

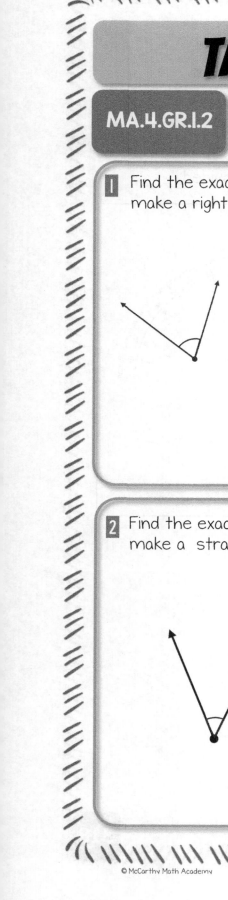
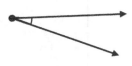

2 Find the exact measure of each angle. Which angles, when added together, make a straight angle? Circle them.

319

TAKING ON THE B.E.S.T.

| **Additive Angles**

1 Find the exact measure of each angle. Which angles, when added together, make a straight angle? Circle them.

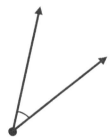  

2 Find the exact measure of each angle. Which angles, when added together, make a right angle? Circle them.

320

TAKING ON THE B.E.S.T.

MA.4.GR.1.2 | **Math Missions** | **Angle Measurements**

PART ONE

Use a protractor to draw two angles. The first angle is 25°, and the second angle is 125°.

PART TWO

Using the two angles above, draw one more angle that when added together would make a straight angle.

PART THREE

Michael says that the angle below has a measure of 46°. What error did Michael make?

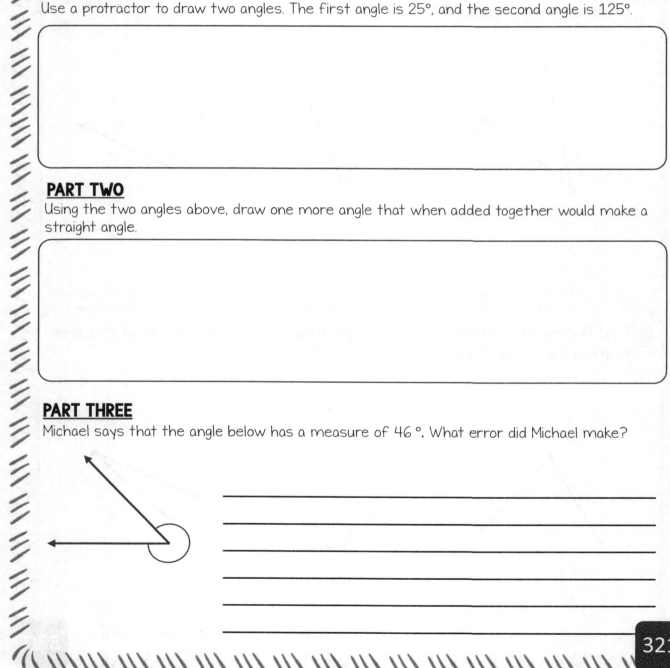

_____
_____
_____
_____
_____
_____

TAKING ON THE B.E.S.T.

| **Math Misconception Mystery**
(PAGE 1)

BEFORE THE VIDEO: Solve the problem on your own.

Use the protractor to find the measure of the indicated angle.

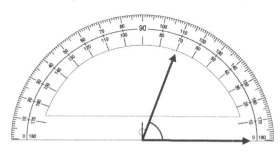

DURING THE VIDEO: Pause after each "character" solves the problem and jot down quick notes to help you remember what they did correctly or incorrectly.

Character #1 _____	Character #2 _____
Character #3 _____	**Character #4** _____

322

TAKING ON THE B.E.S.T.

MA.4.GR.1.2 | Math Misconception Mystery (PAGE 2)

AFTER THE VIDEO: Discuss and analyze their answers.

The most reasonable answer belongs to Character # _____ because

_____

_____

_____

_____

(Justify how this character's work makes sense.)

Let's help the others:

	Character #___:	Character #___:	Character #___:
What did this character do that was correct?			
Identify their error			
What do they need to know to understand for next time?			

323

TAKING ON THE B.E.S.T.

1 Aubrey is adding angles together to create a 160° angle. Select all the angle measures that Aubrey can use to create a 160° angle.

Ⓐ 60° + 60° + 100°
Ⓑ 45° + 45° + 70°
Ⓒ 20° + 60° + 20° + 60°
Ⓓ 75° + 85°

2 Trent is adding angles together to create a 274° angle. Select all the angle measures that Trent can use to create a 274° angle.

Ⓐ 51° + 67° + 157°
Ⓑ 86° + 89° + 99°
Ⓒ 111° + 163°
Ⓓ 65° + 99° + 211°

324

1 Matthew is adding angles together to create a 100° angle. Select all the angle measures that Matthew can use to create a 100° angle.

- Ⓐ 20° + 20° + 30° + 30°
- Ⓑ 15° + 65° + 30°
- Ⓒ 20° + 60° + 40°
- Ⓓ 10° + 20° + 30° + 40°

2 Norman is adding angles together to create a 340° angle. Select all the angle measures that Norman can use to create a 340° angle.

- Ⓐ 73° + 182° + 34° + 49°
- Ⓑ 60° + 60° + 80° + 130°
- Ⓒ 181° + 159°
- Ⓓ 65° + 99° + 176°

TAKING ON THE B.E.S.T.

MA.4.GR.1.3 |  **Video Lesson** | **Find the Measure of Unknown Angles**

---

1 Using the known angle measurements, write an equation to represent < NQO. Then solve.

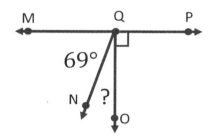

---

2 Using the known angle measurements, write an equation to represent < EFH. Then solve.

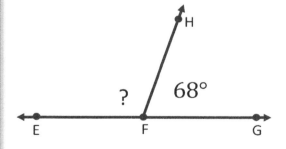

326

© McCarthy Math Academy

TAKING ON THE B.E.S.T.

1 Using the known angle measurements, write an equation to represent < DBC. Then solve.

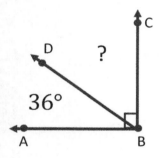

2 Using the known angle measurements, write an equation to represent < HFG. Then solve.

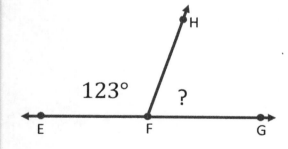

Jake draws two straight lines, $\overline{ST}$ and $\overline{UW}$, which intersect at point L. Using the given angle, find the measure of the three unknown angles. Then, classify each angle as an acute, obtuse, right, or straight angle.

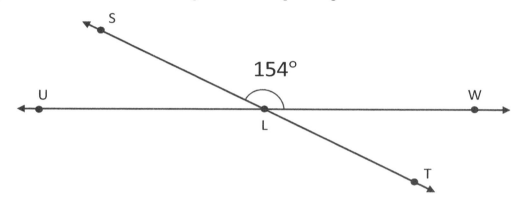

	Angle Measure	Classify the Angle
< SLW		
< WLT		
< TLU		
< ULS		

TAKING ON THE B.E.S.T.

Math Misconception Mystery
(PAGE 1)

BEFORE THE VIDEO: Solve the problem on your own.

Using the known angle measurements, write an equation to find the measure of < RST. Then solve.

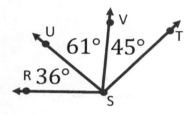

DURING THE VIDEO: Pause after each "character" solves the problem and jot down quick notes to help you remember what they did correctly or incorrectly.

Character #1 _____	Character #2 _____
Character #3 _____	**Character #4** _____

329

TAKING ON THE B.E.S.T.

Math Misconception Mystery (PAGE 2)

AFTER THE VIDEO: Discuss and analyze their answers.

The most reasonable answer belongs to Character # _____ because

_____

_____

_____

_____

(Justify how this character's work makes sense.)

Let's help the others:

	Character #___:	Character #___:	Character #___:
What did this character do that was correct?			
Identify their error			
What do they need to know to understand for next time?			

330

© McCarthy Math Academy

TAKING ON THE B.E.S.T.

MA.4.GR.2.1  **Video Lesson** | **Perimeter and Area Review in Rectangles**

1 Martin buys a blank canvas for his new painting. The dimensions of the canvas are shown below. Find the perimeter and the area of the blank canvas.

12 in

18 in

2 The most common window size has a length of 24 inches and a width of 36 inches. Find the perimeter and the area of a window with the given dimensions.

331

TAKING ON THE B.E.S.T.

1. Iliana purchases new carpet for her room. The dimensions of the carpet are shown below. Find the perimeter and the area of the new carpet.

```
        15 ft
┌──────────────┐
│              │
│              │  13 ft
│              │
└──────────────┘
```

13 ft

15 ft

2. Daniel builds a dance floor with a length of 16 feet and a width of 18 feet. Find the perimeter and the area of Daniel's dance floor.

332

TAKING ON THE B.E.S.T.

1 A flat-screen TV has a perimeter of 298 centimeters. The length of the TV is 95 centimeters.

Write an equation to find the unknown width, W. Then solve.

Write an equation to find the area, A, of the TV. Then solve.

2 Josefina visits a mural downtown. The mural has an area that is 144 square yards. The length of the mural is 9 yards.

Write an equation to find the unknown width, W. Then solve.

Write an equation to find the perimeter, P, of the mural. Then solve.

1 A smart phone has a perimeter of 44 centimeters. The width of the smart phone is 7 centimeters.

Write an equation to find the unknown length, L. Then solve.

Write an equation to find the area, A, of the TV. Then solve.

2 Mr. Thacker has a white board with an area of 24 square feet. The height of the white board is 4 feet.

Write an equation to find the unknown length, L. Then solve.

Write an equation to find the perimeter, P, of the white board. Then solve.

334

TAKING ON THE B.E.S.T.

1 A floor mat has a perimeter of 96 centimeters. The width of 18 centimeters.

Write an equation to find the unknown length, *L*. Then solve.

Write an equation to find the area, *A*, of the floor mat. Then solve.

2 Lucy creates a a square garden with an area of 121 square yards.

Write an equation to find the unknown length, *L*. Then solve.

Write an equation to find the perimeter, *P*, of the garden. Then solve.

TAKING ON THE B.E.S.T.

PART ONE

Draw a rectangle with an perimeter of 140 inches, and a side length of 22 inches. Then, write an equation to determine the missing side length, L, and solve.

PART TWO

Write an equation to find the area, A, of your rectangle. Then, solve.

TAKING ON THE B.E.S.T.

Math Misconception Mystery
(PAGE 1)

BEFORE THE VIDEO: Solve the problem on your own.

> A rectangle has an area of 192 square feet. One of the side lengths is 8 feet. Write an equation to find the perimeter, *P*, of the rectangle.

DURING THE VIDEO: Pause after each "character" solves the problem and jot down quick notes to help you remember what they did correctly or incorrectly.

Character #1 _____	Character #2 _____
Character #3 _____	**Character #4** _____

TAKING ON THE B.E.S.T.

Math Misconception Mystery
(PAGE 2)

AFTER THE VIDEO: Discuss and analyze their answers.

The most reasonable answer belongs to Character # _____ because

_____

_____

_____

_____

(Justify how this character's work makes sense.)

Let's help the others:

	Character #___:	Character #___:	Character #___:
What did this character do that was correct?			
Identify their error			
What do they need to know to understand for next time?			

338

TAKING ON THE B.E.S.T.

1 Two rectangles are shown below. Find the perimeters and areas of each. Then, describe what you notice when you compare their perimeters and areas.

10 cm

12 cm

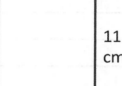

11 cm

11 cm

_____

_____

_____

2 Create another rectangle with the same perimeter as the rectangles above, but a different area.

339

© McCarthy Math Academy

TAKING ON THE B.E.S.T.

1 Two rectangles are shown below. Find the perimeters and areas of each. Then, describe what you notice when you compare their perimeters and areas.

10 cm

18 cm

14 cm

14 cm

_____

_____

_____

2 Create another rectangle with the same perimeter as the rectangles above, but a different area.

340

© McCarthy Math Academy

TAKING ON THE B.E.S.T.

  **Video Lesson** **Rectangles with Same Area, Different Perimeters**

1 Ronnie needs to buy a carpet that will cover an area of 168 square feet. What are two possible lengths and widths that Ronnie could search for to buy a carpet?

2 Two rectangles are shown below. Find the perimeters and areas of each. Then, describe what you notice when you compare their perimeters and areas.

20 in

24 in

12 in

40 in

TAKING ON THE B.E.S.T.

MA.4.GR.2.2 | **Extra Practice #2** | **Rectangles with Same Area, Different Perimeters**

1 A farmer receives 72 square yards of sod. What are two possible lengths and widths the farmer could create when laying down the sod?

2 Two rectangles are shown below. Find the perimeters and areas of each. Then, describe what you notice when you compare their perimeters and areas.

10 in
15 in
5 in
30 in

____

____

____

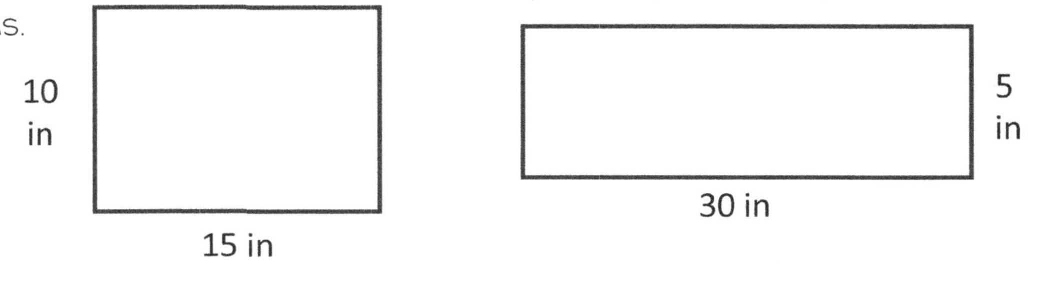

TAKING ON THE B.E.S.T.

| MA.4.GR.2.2 | Math Missions | Real-World Area and Perimeter Problems |

PART ONE

Draw three different rectangles, each with an area of 48 square meters. Label the dimensions of each rectangle.

PART TWO

Using your three different rectangles, describe how the perimeters change as the side lengths change.

_____

_____

_____

_____

_____

TAKING ON THE B.E.S.T.

MA.4.GR.2.2
Math Misconception Mystery
(PAGE 1)

BEFORE THE VIDEO: Solve the problem on your own.

Draw two rectangles that have the same area, but different perimeters.

DURING THE VIDEO: Pause after each "character" solves the problem and jot down quick notes to help you remember what they did correctly or incorrectly.

Character #1 _____

Character #2 _____

Character #3 _____

Character #4 _____

344

TAKING ON THE B.E.S.T.

Math Misconception Mystery
(PAGE 2)

AFTER THE VIDEO: Discuss and analyze their answers.

The most reasonable answer belongs to Character # _____ because

_____

_____

_____

_____

(Justify how this character's work makes sense.)

Let's help the others:

	Character #___:	Character #___:	Character #___:
What did this character do that was correct?			
Identify their error			
What do they need to know to understand for next time?			

345

Matthew tracks his scores on all of his math tests this year. The data he collected is shown below. Use the data to create a stem-and-leaf-plot and line plot.

Matthew's Math Tests Scores	
85	85
76	80
75	93
92	94
94	100
93	94
87	92

Stem	Leaf
Key: 9|2 means 92	

LINE PLOT

346

TAKING ON THE B.E.S.T.

| MA.4.DP.I.I | Extra Practice #1 | Represent Data: Stem-and-Leaf Plots and Line Plots |

Isabel's tracks her scores on all of her science tests this year. The data she collected is shown below. Use the data to create a stem-and-leaf-plot and line plot.

Isabel's Tests Scores	
87	100
75	100
73	83
86	94
86	87
92	85
95	100

Stem	Leaf
Key: 9|2 means 92	

LINE PLOT

MA.4.DP.I.I	 Video Lesson	Represent Data: Stem-and-Leaf Plots and Line Plots

The fourth graders in Mrs. Garcia's class collected data for the amount of time they sleep on average each night. The data they collected is shown below. Use the data to create a stem–and–leaf–plot and line plot.

Time Students Sleep on Average (in hours)	
$7\frac{3}{4}$	$7\frac{3}{4}$
$6\frac{1}{4}$	$6\frac{2}{4}$
$8\frac{2}{4}$	$7\frac{3}{4}$
$6\frac{3}{4}$	$8\frac{1}{4}$
$7\frac{1}{4}$	$8\frac{1}{4}$
$7\frac{2}{4}$	$7\frac{3}{4}$
8	$6\frac{3}{4}$

Stem	Leaf

Key: $6|\frac{3}{4}$ means $6\frac{3}{4}$

LINE PLOT

MA.4.DP.1.1	Extra Practice #2	Represent Data: Stem-and-Leaf Plots and Line Plots

The fourth graders in Mrs. Reyes's class track the number of miles each student walked this week on the track. Use the data to create a stem-and-leaf-plot and line plot.

Miles Walked	
$2\frac{3}{8}$	$2\frac{5}{8}$
$3\frac{1}{8}$	$2\frac{4}{8}$
$3\frac{3}{8}$	$3\frac{6}{8}$
$4\frac{6}{8}$	$3\frac{2}{8}$
$4\frac{2}{8}$	$4\frac{2}{8}$
$1\frac{4}{8}$	$2\frac{5}{8}$
3	$3\frac{1}{8}$

Stem	Leaf

Key: $2|\frac{3}{8}$ means $2\frac{3}{8}$

LINE PLOT

TAKING ON THE B.E.S.T.

| MA.4.DP.1.1 | Math Missions | Represent Data: Stem-and-Leaf Plots and Line Plots |

Write the fractions $\frac{0}{5}, \frac{1}{5}, \frac{2}{5}, \frac{3}{5}$ and $\frac{4}{5}$ on tiny sheets of paper and fold them up. Create random mixed numbers by rolling a dice and picking one fraction, and record the mixed number you created in the chart to the left. Do this 15 times total. Then, create a stem-and-leaf plot and a line plot based on the data.

 $\boxed{\dfrac{3}{5}}$ $= 1\frac{3}{5}$

Random Number Generator		

Stem	Leaf

Key:

LINE PLOT

TAKING ON THE B.E.S.T.

MA.4.DP.1.1 | Math Misconception Mystery (PAGE 1)

BEFORE THE VIDEO: Solve the problem on your own.

Complete the stem-and-leaf plot to display the data:

Terrence's Running Times (in Minutes)	
32	45
33	36
32	45
29	37
28	40

Stem	Leaf

Key:

DURING THE VIDEO: Pause after each "character" solves the problem and jot down quick notes to help you remember what they did correctly or incorrectly.

Character #1 _____

Character #2 _____

Character #3 _____

Character #4 _____

351

TAKING ON THE B.E.S.T.

Math Misconception Mystery
(PAGE 2)

AFTER THE VIDEO: Discuss and analyze their answers.

The most reasonable answer belongs to Character # _____ because	

_____

_____

_____

_____

(Justify how this character's work makes sense.)

Let's help the others:

	Character #___:	Character #___:	Character #___:
What did this character do that was correct?			
Identify their error			
What do they need to know to understand for next time?			

352

Matthew tracks his scores on all of his math tests this year. The data he collected is shown below. Determine the mode, median, and range of Matthew's data.

Matthew's Math Test Scores	
85	85
76	80
75	92
92	94
94	100
93	92
87	

What is the mode of this set of data?

What is the median of this set of data?

What is the range of this set of data?

TAKING ON THE B.E.S.T.

MA.4.DP.I.2	Extra Practice #1	Mode, Median, and Range

Isabel tracks her scores on all of her science tests this year. The data she collected is shown below. Determine the mode, median, and range of Isabel's data.

Isabel's Test Scores	
87	100
75	100
73	83
86	94
86	87
92	85
95	

What is the mode of this set of data?

What is the median of this set of data?

What is the range of this set of data?

TAKING ON THE B.E.S.T.

  Video Lesson | Mode, Median, and Range

The fourth graders in Mrs. Garcia's class collected data for the amount of time they sleep on average each night. The data they collected is shown below. Determine the mode, median, and range of this data.

Time Students Sleep on Average (in hours)	
$7\frac{3}{4}$	$7\frac{3}{4}$
$6\frac{1}{4}$	$6\frac{2}{4}$
$8\frac{2}{4}$	$7\frac{3}{4}$
$6\frac{3}{4}$	$8\frac{1}{4}$
$7\frac{1}{4}$	$8\frac{1}{4}$
$7\frac{2}{4}$	$7\frac{3}{4}$
8	

What is the mode of this set of data?

What is the median of this set of data?

What is the range of this set of data?

TAKING ON THE B.E.S.T.

| MA.4.DP.1.2 | Extra Practice #2 | Mode, Median, and Range |

The fourth graders in Mrs. Reyes's class tracked the number of miles each student walked this week on the track. Determine the mode, median, and range of this data

Miles Walked	
$2\frac{3}{8}$	$2\frac{5}{8}$
$3\frac{1}{8}$	$2\frac{4}{8}$
$3\frac{3}{8}$	$3\frac{6}{8}$
$4\frac{6}{8}$	$3\frac{2}{8}$
$5\frac{2}{8}$	$4\frac{2}{8}$
$1\frac{4}{8}$	$2\frac{5}{8}$
5	

What is the mode of this set of data?

What is the median of this set of data?

What is the range of this set of data?

356

© McCarthy Math Academy

TAKING ON THE B.E.S.T.

  Video Lesson | **Mode**

Analyze each data set. Determine whether there is no mode, one mode, or more than one mode. Then, find the range and median of the data.

1 17 fourth grade students were asked to rate how much they enjoy math on a scale from one to ten. Here is the data collected: 10, 9, 5, 6, 9, 8, 7, 6, 1, 2, 7, 3, 7, 1, 7, 6, 6.

2 Issac has 13 pieces of string. He measures each string to the nearest $\frac{1}{8}$ inch, and then he records them on the stem–and–leaf plot below.

Stem	Leaf
5	$\frac{1}{8}$ $\frac{2}{8}$ $\frac{4}{8}$
6	$\frac{3}{8}$ $\frac{4}{8}$ $\frac{5}{8}$ $\frac{7}{8}$
7	$\frac{1}{8}$ $\frac{2}{8}$ $\frac{3}{8}$ $\frac{4}{8}$ $\frac{6}{8}$ $\frac{7}{8}$

Key: $5 | \frac{3}{8} = 5\frac{3}{8}$

3 Mr. Alexander surveys the ages of the 19 students in his class. His data is shown on the line plot below.

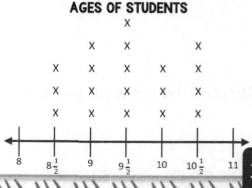

AGES OF STUDENTS

357

© McCarthy Math Academy

TAKING ON THE B.E.S.T.

MA.4.DP.1.2	Extra Practice #3	Mode

Analyze each data set. Determine whether there is no mode, one mode, or more than one mode. Then, find the range and median of the data.

1 21 fourth grade students were asked to rate how much they enjoy reading on a scale from one to ten. Here is the data collected: 2, 4, 6, 2, 3, 5, 2, 8, 10, 10, 8, 10, 1, 4, 6, 7, 8, 9, 8, 2, 8

2 23 students are playing a game at recess. They track their results on the stem-and-leaf plot below.

Stem	Leaf
1	0, 1, 2, 3, 7, 8, 9
2	1, 2, 3, 4, 5
3	6, 7, 7, 8
4	0, 2, 3, 4, 6, 7, 8

Key: 1|0 = 10

3 Mrs. Clarkson's class tracks the amount of water they each consumed the day before (in gallons). Their data is shown on the line plot below.

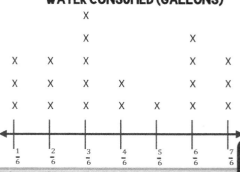

WATER CONSUMED (GALLONS)

TAKING ON THE B.E.S.T.

| MA.4.DP.1.2 | Math Missions | Mode, Median, and Range in A Data Set |

Write the fractions $\frac{0}{4}, \frac{1}{4}, \frac{2}{4}$, and $\frac{3}{4}$ on tiny sheets of paper and fold them up. Create random mixed numbers by rolling a dice and picking one fraction, and record the mixed number you created in the chart to the left. Do this 15 times total. Then, create a stem-and-leaf plot and a line plot based on the data. Finally, determine the mode, range, and median of your data set.

 $\boxed{\dfrac{2}{4}}$ $= 1\frac{2}{4}$

Random Number Generator		

Stem	Leaf

Key:

LINE PLOT

What is the mode of this set of data?

What is the median of this set of data?

What is the range of this set of data?

359

TAKING ON THE B.E.S.T.

Math Misconception Mystery
(PAGE I)

BEFORE THE VIDEO: Solve the problem on your own.

Determine the mode, median, and range for the data set below.

Terrence's Running Times (in Minutes)	
32	45
33	36
32	45
29	37
28	40
41	

DURING THE VIDEO: Pause after each "character" solves the problem and jot down quick notes to help you remember what they did correctly or incorrectly.

Character #1 _____

Character #2 _____

Character #3 _____

Character #4 _____

360

TAKING ON THE B.E.S.T.

Math Misconception Mystery
(PAGE 2)

AFTER THE VIDEO: Discuss and analyze their answers.

The most reasonable answer belongs to Character # _____ because

_____

_____

_____

_____

(Justify how this character's work makes sense.)

Let's help the others:

	Character #___:	Character #___:	Character #___:
What did this character do that was correct?			
Identify their error			
What do they need to know to understand for next time?			

361

TAKING ON THE B.E.S.T.

  **Video Lesson** **Solve Real-World Problems with Stem-and-Leaf Plots**

9 students are playing a game at recess. They track their results on the stem-and-leaf plot below.

Stem	Leaf
1	3, 7
2	1, 5
3	6, 7, 7
4	4, 8
Key: 1|0 = 10	

1 How much greater is the median number of points than the least number of points?

2 The students are trying to score a combined total of 300 points. How many more points do they need to reach this score?

362

TAKING ON THE B.E.S.T.

| **Extra Practice #1** | **Solve Real-World Problems with Stem-and-Leaf Plots**

A police officer tracks the speeds of oncoming traffic. He tracks the data he collects using this stem-and-leaf plot.

Stem	Leaf
2	2, 3, 5, 9
3	0, 1, 4, 8, 8, 9
4	0, 0, 1, 2, 3

Key: 2|0 = 10

1 The speed limit is 30 miles per hour. How much greater or less is the median speed compared to the speed limit?

2 Every vehicle that is traveling 10 or more miles per hour over the speed limit receives a $75 speed limit fine. How much money in speeding fines will the drivers in this data set pay?

TAKING ON THE B.E.S.T.

A grocery store employee weighs bags of grapes in the produce department. The weight of each bag is tracked on the line plot below.

WEIGHT OF BAGS OF GRAPES (IN POUNDS)

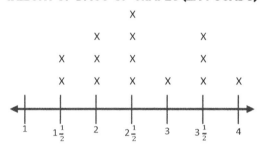

1 What is the combined weight of the bags that weigh $2\frac{1}{2}$ pounds?

2 A customer selects one of the bags of grapes to purchase, and now the total weight of grapes remaining is 33 pounds. Which bag did the customer select?

364

TAKING ON THE B.E.S.T.

MA.4.DP.I.3 | **Extra Practice #2** | **Solve Real-World Problems with Line Plots**

Ms. Gaspy gives her students a math quiz with 6 questions on it. She tracks the number of questions each student answers correctly on the line plot below.

NUMBER OF CORRECT MATH PROBLEMS

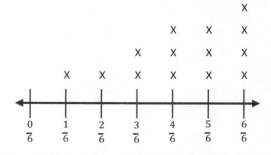

1 How many students answered more than half of the questions correctly?

2 Mrs. Gaspy's students created a goal before taking the test. They wanted to answer a combined amount of 60 questions correctly. Did they achieve their goal?

365

TAKING ON THE B.E.S.T.

| MA.4.DP.I.3 | Math Missions | Solve Real-World Problems with Data Sets |

Measure the length of 11 books to the nearest quarter inch. Track the lengths in the table. Then, complete a stem-and-leaf plot and a line plot based on your data set. Finally, answer the questions based on your data set.

Book Lengths

Stem	Leaf

Key:

LINE PLOT

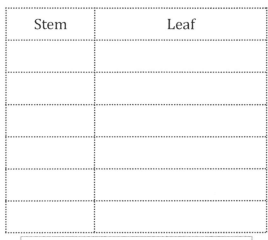

What is the range, median, and mode of your data?

Create your own question based on your data set and solve.

What is the sum of the three greatest lengths of books?

366

TAKING ON THE B.E.S.T.

MA.4.DP.I.3	Math Misconception Mystery (PAGE I)

BEFORE THE VIDEO: Solve the problem on your own.

Keisha tracks the time she spends practicing her multiplication facts each day and records it on the line plot below. What is the difference of the longest time and the second shortest time that Keisha practices her multiplication facts?

Time Spent Practicing Multiplication Facts (in hours)

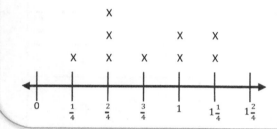

DURING THE VIDEO: Pause after each "character" solves the problem and jot down quick notes to help you remember what they did correctly or incorrectly.

Character #1 _____	Character #2 _____
Character #3 _____	**Character #4** _____

367

TAKING ON THE B.E.S.T.

Math Misconception Mystery (PAGE 2)

AFTER THE VIDEO: Discuss and analyze their answers.

The most reasonable answer belongs to Character # _____ because

_____

_____

_____

_____

(Justify how this character's work makes sense.)

Let's help the others:

	Character #___:	Character #___:	Character #___:
What did this character do that was correct?			
Identify their error			
What do they need to know to understand for next time?			

368